MILLENNIAL RANGER

Spiritual Survival
while Surviving

Christopher L. Watkins

WESTBOW PRESS
A DIVISION OF THOMAS NELSON
& ZONDERVAN

Copyright © 2019 Christopher L. Watkins.

All rights reserved. No part of this book may be used or reproduced by any means, graphic, electronic, or mechanical, including photocopying, recording, taping or by any information storage retrieval system without the written permission of the author except in the case of brief quotations embodied in critical articles and reviews.

This book is a work of non-fiction. Unless otherwise noted, the author and the publisher make no explicit guarantees as to the accuracy of the information contained in this book and in some cases, names of people and places have been altered to protect their privacy.

WestBow Press books may be ordered through booksellers or by contacting:

WestBow Press
A Division of Thomas Nelson & Zondervan
1663 Liberty Drive
Bloomington, IN 47403
www.westbowpress.com
1 (866) 928-1240

Because of the dynamic nature of the Internet, any web addresses or links contained in this book may have changed since publication and may no longer be valid. The views expressed in this work are solely those of the author and do not necessarily reflect the views of the publisher, and the publisher hereby disclaims any responsibility for them.

Any people depicted in stock imagery provided by Getty Images are models, and such images are being used for illustrative purposes only.
Certain stock imagery © Getty Images.

All Scripture quotations are taken from the New King James Version®. Copyright © 1982 by Thomas Nelson. Used by permission. All rights reserved

ISBN: 978-1-9736-7435-1 (sc)
ISBN: 978-1-9736-7437-5 (hc)
ISBN: 978-1-9736-7436-8 (e)

Library of Congress Control Number: 2019914170

Print information available on the last page.

WestBow Press rev. date: 09/30/2019

For my lovely wife, Crystal and our two
amazing children, Jakob and Gracie:
You are true blessings and the
wind beneath my wings.

CONTENTS

Acknowledgments ix
Preface xi
Introduction xv
Chapter 1   Millennials at War 1
Chapter 2   Signs and Revelation 9
Chapter 3   Survival Pattern 24
Chapter 4   Food 33
Chapter 5   Water 53
Chapter 6   Shelter 65
Chapter 7   Fire 80
Chapter 8   Signal 95
Chapter 9   First Aid 108
Chapter 10 Field Craft 122
Chapter 11 Equipment 135
Chapter 12 Be Prepared 148
Chapter 13 Weapons 174
Chapter 14 Family and Community 189
Chapter 15 Ultimate Survival 200
About the Author 209

ACKNOWLEDGMENTS

Special thanks to Caleb Perkins of Caleb Perkins Ministries, Nathan Lyons, and Chaplain Phil Kramer for your brotherhood and edification. Thanks to all my family and friends who have always encouraged me to write this book. I would also like to thank the men and women serving in the armed forces who keep the United States safe. God bless my beloved 75th Ranger Regiment, and God bless the United States' heroes in the sky. Rangers lead the way!

PREFACE

And I saw the beast, the kings of the earth, and their armies, gathered together to make war against Him who sat on the horse and against His army.

—Revelation 19:19

Dawn is creeping closer as the sun begins to rise. Even though it is already hot from the night before, the new rays of light begin to warm the earth. Two snipers begin stalking toward what seems to be a savvy over watch position in the tall grass. They are alongside a berm near the edge of a small Afghanistan village. The previous forty-eight hours have been spent with hardly any food or water as the hot July sun scorched everything in the desert. The snipers are fatigued from two days of living on top of a mud hut occupied by United States Marines. They are now grateful finally to be in motion. The two men have been conditioned to deal with this stress-inducing environment where only the daring and the bold can endure. With Spartan-like mind-sets, the snipers are ready for anything. Not too far away is the main fighting force of the other rangers, who also thrive on the same mental standing.

Brilliant light now begins to flood the area. By now the ranger snipers are crawling into their final position; daylight is not their ally. The sniper team leader delivers his status over the radio, saying that the elite two-man team is now in position. The snipers wait. Moments later the platoon sergeant of the main element passes down his sitrep to the whole fighting force. The temperature continues to rise at a steady pace. Brave, disciplined men now inhabit the area, patiently waiting for an indication that their target is arriving.

Off in the distance is a motorized buzzing sound that appears to be drifting closer. Everyone hears it. At first the noise doesn't sound like much of anything. As the curious sound swiftly echoes past, the Doppler effect translates that there is a moving dirt bike in the area. The bike zips by once again. The driver shows way too much interest in what is going on within the area of operation. The closest squad of rangers reveal themselves from their covered and concealed positions. They approach the driver and his tandem passenger with the intent of detaining and questioning them. The squad is now in the open. Each man has his weapon oriented in its respective direction to ensure that every possible area around the squad is covered.

The two snipers begin to move toward the top of the berm to gain eyes on the situation. As both men advance just short of the top, there is the distinct and familiar sound of snaps and cracks; rounds begin to make their impacts around the two-man team. In an instant, the whole fighting force is now engaged in a massive firefight with enemy forces. Amid chaotic explosions and gunshots from all directions, the sniper team leader feels a hard kick against his left foot. While prone, he turns around and yells, "What's up?" There's no one behind him. It is at this point that the buzzing noise has caught up with his brain's ability to register and process the information. Time slows down. It could have been shrapnel. Most likely he has been shot. Either way, the burning, throbbing pain begins to become more and more apparent.

The snipers convey the injury over the radio and add that they are capable of movement. While under covering fire from the main force, the snipers bound and sprint toward the main body. Farther down the berm, the snipers dive over the top of the berm in a desperate attempt to avoid getting shot again. Once they traverse to the other side, they begin to slide down a steep, slick wall of mud. The wall leads to knee-high water polluted with the fecal matter of the local villagers. The soldier with the wounded foot begins to grimace at the excruciating pain. The dirty water has flooded his boots and made its way into the gash located on the outside of his left foot.

Determined, the snipers begin to travel through the irrigation canal toward their comrades. After vigorously fighting through dense vegetation and a volley of RPGs and bullets traveling overhead, the two men meet up with one of the medics at the scene. Scrupulous medical aid is provided to the injured sniper, and both men are now able to join their buddies behind cover.

The whole fighting force is now regrouped and continues to fight off the enemy. Two other members of the elite fighting force have also been shot. As the medevac arrives, the sniper with the shot foot takes a moment to thank God for His protection and prays that He will continue to bless him and his brothers still engaged in the battle.

INTRODUCTION

I truly believe that the events in my life that have involved struggle were conquered by my faith in God and the stubborn will to survive that He has conferred upon me. "Faith without works is dead" (James 2:17). In addition to all the previous training I received through the military, the mental attitude that I have developed throughout the course of my life played a huge role in my survival in many other risky situations. Because of this mentality, I'm ready to survive.

    The skills that I have acquired through my career as a ranger would have done me no justice whatsoever had I not possessed the resilient desire to survive and trust in God. There are multitudes of people who have no practical training at all who have made it out of other life-threatening situations solely because on their will to make it out alive. I believe a large part of this is on account of God's protection and working miracles and the fact that He created us to thrive (Psalm 92:12–13). This should be pretty reassuring news for those of you who have no idea how to react in a treacherous setting. However, this mental attitude must be obtained—it does not happen automatically every time death stares you directly in the eyes.

With the mental ability to navigate through stress, proper training and practice will increase your survivability immensely when you are challenged by a disaster. The knowledge of survival skills will give you the invaluable ability to extinguish fear as you step into the darkness of the unknown, for God did not give us the spirit of fear (2 Timothy 1:7).

Your readiness to combating the aftermath of chaos will award you with self-confidence and allow you to thrive by your wits. In order to know how to survive, you must develop and master what the military calls a pattern for survival. The basic survival pattern includes food, water, shelter, fire, first aid, and signaling.

In *Millennial Ranger: Spiritual Survival while Surviving*, I will reveal these patterns and provide my input based on the training I have undergone while serving in the Special Operations community as a ranger and as a sniper. I will also share with you my views on preparedness as a Christian.

For simplicity's sake, all scripture references are taken from the New King James Version of the Bible. (Copyright © 1982 by Thomas Nelson, Inc. Used by permission. All rights reserved.)

It's important to remember that all things are possible with God who gives you strength (Philippians 4:13). In the book of Revelation in the Bible, which is the Word of God, the end of the present age is revealed as God will bring His kingdom to earth. Jesus is coming back; His return will be sooner than you or I may even think! Jesus says, "Behold, I am coming as a thief" (Revelation 16:15)!

This is not just a book about how to build fires and find food, although these topics will be covered. This is a book about finding yourself in Christ and figuring out what God's will is for you on this earth, because God wants us to be able to survive. "For you have need of endurance, so that after you have done the will of God, you may receive the promise" (Hebrews 10:36).

However, no matter how equipped and prepared you are to survive planet Earth, without Jesus you are destined for failure and doomed to eternal damnation, because this is not your permanent residence—heaven is. With that, I hope *Millennial Ranger* will provide you with the knowledge and inspiration to survive both physically and spiritually.

> ***"For the wages of sin is death, but the gift of God is eternal life in Christ Jesus our Lord" (Romans 6:23).***

1

MILLENNIALS AT WAR

On September 11, 2001, I was sitting in Spanish II class at my school. It was my junior year in high school, and I had barely passed Spanish I the previous year—for the second time, that is. I was starting to nod off when the teacher stopped in the middle of the class because of a phone call from the office. Once she was finished with the phone call, she let us know that there had been a terrorist attack on the World Trade Center; terrorists had crashed planes into the two large buildings in the middle of New York City. At the time, I had no idea what any of these things meant. But I became more infuriated over the next few days as I developed a more educated understanding of the situation.

As we all know by now, this event sparked the United States to declare a global war on terrorism (GWOT). This war launched our fighting forces (boots on the ground) into two different campaigns known as Operation Iraqi Freedom in Iraq and Operation Enduring Freedom in Afghanistan. Many of us have always been proud to be Americans our whole lives, but it was this event that eventually sparked a sense of duty and adventure for the men and women of the millennial generation: Generation Y.

   One of the things I have taken a lot of pride in is the ability to differentiate myself from typical people of my generation. Technically I would be considered a millennial. Although I deny this accusation regularly, I'm definitely not a member of Generation X. And then there is Generation Z, which I'd like to mention is the *last* letter of the alphabet. I prefer to pool myself in with the unique category of what I like to call Generation GWOT, which is mainly made up of millennials anyway. Be that as it may, because of this distinct and self-appointed difference, I immediately felt honor bound to serve my country and would later become what the US Army calls a three-time volunteer.

   During my coming of age and entrance into the military, I was continuously haunted by my past. I had had a great childhood. Like every other kid of my generation, I fought dragons and dreamed of being involved in something larger than myself as I ran around in kid-size BDUs (battle dress uniforms) and dog tags. More importantly, I have called myself a Christian ever since I can remember—probably since age five or so. I remember taking pride in being part of a churchgoing family and spending time with other churchgoing families. We took vacations together. We slept in our Michigan basement when the power went out. We saw local semipro hockey games. We grew up playing sports. We went to the lake to spend time at the beach. We were Boy Scouts who roamed the woods with pocketknives and hatchets and started fires at a young age. We drank water straight from the hose when we were thirsty.

Eventually these things changed, like many things do. We left the place where I'd spent most of my childhood days and the very beginning of my teenage years to move to Hampton Roads, Virginia. I was fifteen and had no idea just how much my life would change over the next couple of years. Despite having to adjust to a different state in the South, where no one knows how to drive in the snow, I noticed how much of the area was militarily driven. I was intrigued. Seeing people in their BDUs shopping or stopping for gas on the way to or from work was something that I had never experienced before.

Within that first year or so in Virginia, my parents separated and eventually divorced. All this occurred around the time of the September 11 terrorist attacks. Like many of my brothers with whom I would eventually serve in the army, I was a child of divorce and just wanted to move on. All I knew was what I'd left behind; there was nowhere to go but forward. Eventually I would be destined to look back and regard these events as blessings in disguise, despite my fury that fueled a rebellious and hardheaded spirit.

I could not graduate high school fast enough to join the United States Army. Already knowing that four more years of school with people my own age who thought that they knew how the world worked but didn't seemed very unappealing to me. I had no desires or dreams of scholarships. The sheer thought of college made me sick to my stomach. So that next year, toward the end of my junior year, at age seventeen, I signed up for the delayed-entry program. I was determined to see how the world really was—and hopefully kill some terrorists along the way.

I ended up getting an 11X contract to join the US Army with the guarantee that I would be participating in the RIP (Ranger Indoctrination Program). Of course, I had to complete army basic training and Airborne School first. Enlisting and agreeing to go through infantry school during basic training, Airborne School, and RIP would make me a three-time volunteer of hazardous duties from the start. I originally wanted to go into the Special Forces 18X program. My parents made me sit down with a family friend who was an officer in the Special Forces. When he asked me why I wanted to go into the SF, I immediately responded, "To serve in war and kill bad guys." He almost as quickly responded that I should go into the Seventy-Fifth Ranger Regiment if that was the case. He was a graduate of the US Army Ranger School and told me about the rigorous training it requires. I was instantly intrigued and within a few weeks had my contract thanks to my recruiter.

My senior year was a pain because all I wanted to do was party with my friends and slack off, and at times I did. But despite my recently acquired rebelliousness, I knew that to get into the army I had to graduate high school first. Luckily, having played soccer my whole life and playing on the high school team helped keep me focused and in shape. I also spent time in the woods any chance I got. And, yes, I played plenty of video games too.

Well, eventually I graduated high school, and before summer was completely over, I found myself getting on a bus headed to Fort Benning, Georgia, home of the infantry, to begin the adventure of a lifetime. One thing I picked up on instantly during my ride there was that I was at the beginning of a four-year enlistment surrounded by a bunch of people my own age who thought that they knew how the world worked but didn't—myself included. We all were destined to find out eventually, though.

Army basic training had its share of challenges but was not extremely difficult. I would go as far as to say it was a bit of a joke, although I was a horrible shot with a rifle. Airborne School was about what I'd expected, and that wasn't impossible either. By the time I got to RIP, I had already built some confidence in myself and was ready for the month-long rigorous training. I knew this would be one of the greatest challenges of my life, which it turned out to be.

Eventually I made it to my beloved Third Ranger Battalion. The men from my platoon welcomed me with open arms. That is, my arms were open with my hands planted firmly on the ground and my feet elevated on some lockers while I was doing push-ups to the sound of perplexed confusion and yelling, with others asking me why I was so "ate up." This is the standard, and looking back, I wouldn't have it any other way. I worked hard to get there, and I was sure going to work hard to stay there—with the typical speed bumps along the way.

People say that after you leave the military, you only remember the good times and none of the bad times and always wish that you could return, even for just one more day. Those people are right. I thoroughly loved being a ranger. The gut check of Ranger School happened to give me some of my favorite memories of my entire enlistment.

I went to Ranger School as a private first class

within my first year in battalion. With one combat deployment to Afghanistan under my belt already, which earned me a Combat Infantrymen's Badge, I was feeling on top of the world. I seriously thrived and went "indigenous" during my stay at Ranger School; I took to heart the practice of embracing adversity and sometimes felt a smile on my face when I faced an obstacle. Other times I repeated in prayer, "Please, God, just let me get through one more thing." God answers prayers, and eventually I became a graduate of the United States Army Ranger School, which earned me the right to wear a Ranger tab on my uniform.

As I progressed through the ranks over the next several years, I moved on from the line company to become a dog handler and then eventually a sniper. I noticed that my rebellious spirit had started to decline. I gave God greater thought. I credit that in part to some good buddies of mine who are sincere Christians. Every once in a while, they would pull me out of dark places and invite me to church. I also credit that to meeting my wife, who became—and who still is—a great driving force in my life. She is the one whom God sent to keep me on the straight and narrow.

I had served seven combat deployments with Third Ranger Battalion by the end of my enlistment, three to Afghanistan and four to Iraq. On my seventh deployment, which was to Afghanistan in 2009, I had my wife waiting for me, and she was three months pregnant with our first child. Like I said before, I have always been a Christian, and when I was shot, I was having conversations with God through internal prayer—and through it all I had a sense of calmness come over me. I knew that I would be all right, and I knew that I was going back to my wife, and I knew I would be there for my son. After that last deployment, I was retired because of the injuries I sustained from my gunshot wound. And in case you are wondering, yes, I did keep my foot, although there was a serious concern about infection.

It wasn't until several months later when I was cleaning and preparing my gear to give back to the army that I realized just how much God has blessed me. The back of my body armor plate carrier had two streaks, one across the top and one across the bottom, where two bullet rounds had traveled and cut through the material. After further investigation, I discovered that another round had pierced through the gauze in my personal medical pouch. Yet another blessing in disguise. "For no weapon formed against you shall prosper" (Isaiah 54:17).

Although the time spent serving in the military makes up the formative years for veterans who serve in young adulthood, the next , which starts outside the military, is what really makes us or breaks us. Within the first few years of having done different jobs outside of the military and now with two kids in our family (a son and a daughter), I was impressed with the thought that I was no longer beholden to the military or to the men whom I once fought alongside. I was now honor bound to raise godly children and share a God-fearing relationship with my wife. I was charged with the responsibility of their physical and spiritual protection as head of household. Although I still would do anything for the brothers I once served with, my main objective had been transformed completely to focus on the survivability of my family.

Because of my mission as a Christian and as a father, I did what any other person in my situation would do: seek a more meaningful relationship with God. The best way to do that is to study—not just skim through, but sincerely take in—the Word of God. The other part of it is to communicate with God through prayer—lots and lots of prayer.

Not long after I got out of the military, my wife gave me one of the greatest Christmas gifts I would ever receive: my Bible. This was a black leather-bound Bible that I was determined to read cover to cover. At the time, I had never done this before in my whole life; I was merely a lukewarm Christian. The fact that I hadn't taken the time to read the entire Bible was something that I was ashamed of. To reflect on the few times that I could have been killed in combat or even in training without having read the whole Word of God gave me shivers down my spine. One of my buddies from the army once upon a time suggested that the best book to start with was the book of Revelation. I'm glad I followed that suggestion. Because of the message of this book, I was inspired to consider what's going on in the world that I would have otherwise given no regard to.

2

SIGNS AND REVELATION

As my surroundings changed, so did my influences. Not only did I reflect on the things that I have been a part of in modern events, but also I gradually took a keen interest in historical events. In addition, I eventually started to notice the things going on around me as I became more politically aware. And I saw things going on around the world through a different lens. Finally, it dawned on me that there are events that are occurring and continue to occur that are on a biblical level. As I increasingly sharpened my knowledge and studied the Word of God, my faith was supplemented at an exponential rate like never before. I was going through a transformation in the Spirit.

In Matthew 24:3, after Jesus predicts the destruction of the temple, Jesus's disciples ask, "Tell us, when will these things be? And what will be the sign of Your coming, and the end of the age?" Then, "Jesus answered and said to them: 'Take heed that no one deceives you. For many will come in My name, saying, "I am the Christ," and will deceive many. And you will hear of wars and rumors of wars. See that you are not troubled; for all these things must come to pass, but the end is not yet. For nation will rise against nation, and kingdom against kingdom. And there will be famines, pestilences, and earthquakes in various places. All these are the beginning of sorrows'" (Matthew 24:4-7).

Jesus answers His disciples by explaining that there will be people pretending to be Christ. There will be wars and rumors of wars. Jesus tells His disciples that there will be famines and pestilence and earthquakes. Jesus even says that these things must come to pass, but the end is not yet. Take another look at Matthew 24:8: "All these are the beginning of sorrows." All of these horrible things are not even the tribulation but are events leading up to the tribulation. Immediately in Matthew 24:9, Jesus goes on to say, "Then they will deliver you up to tribulation and kill you, and you will be hated by all nations for My name's sake."

So, in Matthew 24:4-8, I believe Jesus is talking about things that are leading up to the seven years of tribulation. In Matthew 24:9-14, I believe that Jesus is actually describing the first three and a half years of the tribulation. Matthew 24:15-28 is the great tribulation and the second three and a half years of the total seven-year tribulation. Finally, in Matthew 24:29-31 is the coming of the Son of man (Jesus), *after* the tribulation of those days. Nowhere in the Bible does it say that Jesus will return, rapture us, leave, and then return a second time after the tribulation for His final judgment. This is important because if someone is claiming to be Christ, you will know better and not be deceived.

So where does that put us in the grand scheme of things? I believe that we are living in the time of wars and rumors of wars. I believe that there are famines and pestilences going on globally. The rate of earthquake activity around the world has been increasing. Even in the United States, the Yellowstone volcano is past due for an eruption, and when it erupts, it will wipe out a large portion of the United States. So, yes, I believe that we are approaching the end of times that Jesus spoke of to His disciples. I believe that people throughout the United States are living like those in the days of Noah before the Flood. I believe that many people are partaking in idolatry and child sacrifices. How many people don't practice faith in God but are consumed with all things of the flesh, such as money and technology? How many babies have been aborted across the United States over the years? People are drinking and marrying, going on with their normal daily lives, and are not giving these things an inkling of a second thought.

> **The sun shall be turned into darkness,**
> **And the moon into blood,**
> **Before the coming of the great and awesome day of the Lord.**
>
> **—Joel 2:31**

> **I will show wonders in heaven above**
> **And signs in the earth beneath:**
> **Blood and fire and vapor of smoke.**

> **The sun shall be turned into darkness,
> And the moon into blood,
> Before the coming of the great and awesome day of the Lord
> And it shall come to pass
> That whoever calls on the name of the Lord
> Shall be saved.**
>
> —Acts 2:19-21

In 2014-15 there were four blood moons that took place, which is called a blood moon tetrad. A blood moon tetrad is when four consecutive total lunar eclipses happen in a series. Total lunar eclipses result in the moon appearing to have a red/orangish tint, which is called a blood moon. The interesting thing about the tetrad is that each one took place during a major Jewish holiday:

- April 15, 2014, Jewish Passover—lunar eclipse
- October 8, 2014, Feast of Tabernacles—lunar eclipse
- March 20, 2015, Jewish New Year for Kings—solar eclipse
- April 4, 2015, Jewish Passover—lunar eclipse
- September 13, 2015, Feast of Trumpets—solar eclipse
- September 28, 2015, Feast of Tabernacles—lunar eclipse

In 2033-34, the next blood moon tetrad will take place during major Jewish holidays yet again:

- April 14, 2033, Jewish Passover—lunar eclipse
- October 8, 2033, Sukkot—lunar eclipse
- March 20, 2034, solar eclipse—during blood moon tetrad

- April 3, 2034, Passover—lunar eclipse
- September 28, 2034, Jewish Passover—lunar eclipse

So, you might be wondering, *Okay, so do I have until 2033 or 2034 at least to get ready for the return of Christ?* Well, in my mind, maybe and maybe not. Does God have to wait on a sign that we already know is coming? Why would God be bound to something that humankind has calculated? Don't you know that God created the universe and that He does things according to His perfect plan? "God does whatever pleases Him" (Psalm 135:6). Doesn't the Bible say that the day of the Lord so comes as a thief in the night (1 Thessalonians 5:2)? By the sixth seal, there will still be signs in the sky of blood moons (Revelation 6:12).

> **Now a great sign appeared in heaven: a woman clothed with the sun, with the moon under her feet, and on her head a garland of twelve stars. Then being with child, she cried out in labor and in pain to give birth.**
>
> **And another sign appeared in heaven: behold, a great, fiery red dragon having seven heads and ten horns, and seven diadems on his heads. His tail drew a third of the stars of heaven and threw them to the earth. And the dragon stood before the woman who was ready to give birth, to devour her Child as soon as it was born. She bore a male Child who was to rule all the nations with a rod of iron. And her Child was**

> **caught up to God and His throne. Then the woman fled into the wilderness, where she has a place prepared by God, that they should feed her there for one thousand two hundred and sixty days. (Revelation 12:1-6)**
>
> **And there will be signs in the sun, in the moon, and in the stars; and on the earth distress of nations, with perplexity, the sea and the waves roaring. (Luke 21:25)**

In 2015 the star of Bethlehem was visible for the first time in over two thousand years. You may remember reading about the previous time it was visible in the Bible, around the time when Jesus was born. On September 23, 2017, there was an occurrence that only happens once every seven thousand years. When the constellations Leo and Virgo lined up with the sun and the moon, Jupiter stayed in the abdominal area of Virgo for the course of nine months. The moon appeared to be at the feet of the constellation Virgo, and the sun was near the constellation as well. Jupiter is also called the King Planet as it is the largest planet in our solar system. The last time this event happened was approximately 962 years before Adam and Eve were created.

So, within a two-year period, we as a world witnessed a sign in the sky that symbolizes the birth of Jesus in Bethlehem and a sign that represents the events described in Revelation 12. Revelation 12 is the description of Satan rebelling in heaven and being cast out with a third of the angels. We also know by reading the book of Genesis that the fallen angels bred with the women of earth. This was an attempt by Satan to destroy the Davidic bloodline that would eventually bring forth Jesus born of the Virgin Mary. By breeding with the women of earth, the fallen angels created the Nephilim. When the Nephilim were created, the world was full of sin and God brought the Flood on to destroy all these abominations. When considering these atrocities, remember what Jesus said in Matthew 24:37, "But as the days of Noah were, so also will the coming of the Son of Man be." Now consider what the Bible has to say regarding mystery Babylon during the end times. "Now the great city was divided into three parts, and the cities of the nations fell. And great Babylon was remembered before God, to give her the cup of wine of the fierceness of His wrath" (Revelation 16:19).

August 21, 2017, was what some people call the Great American Eclipse, in which the path of the moon could be viewed throughout the United States of America. In 2024, seven years later, there will be another similar eclipse that will move across the United States in the opposite direction. The visible path, as drawn on a map, will intersect, forming an *x* over the New Madrid Fault Line, which is in the southeastern part of the United States. Opposite that area in the northwestern part of the United States is the volcano at Yellowstone National Park that is way past due for an eruption. The blast from this super volcano will send ash for thousands of miles and will cause catastrophic damage throughout the region. It will damage crops and destroy buildings. How is this important? Well, if you were to draw a line from the northern border to the southern border of both locations, it would seemingly and blatantly divide the United States into thirds. According to the book of Revelation, this event will take place after the seventh bowl has been poured, resulting in the total destruction of Babylon.

> **Then one of the seven angels who had the seven bowls came and talked with me, saying to me, "Come, I will show you the judgment of the great harlot who sits on many waters, with whom the kings of the earth committed fornication, and the inhabitants of the earth were made drunk with the wine of her fornication." … And on her forehead a name was written:** MYSTERY, BABYLON THE GREAT, THE MOTHER OF HARLOTS AND OF THE ABOMINATIONS OF THE EARTH. **(Revelation 17:1–2, 5)**

Many scholars believe that the United States of America is the mystery Babylon that is described in the Bible. Some also believe that, more specifically, it could be New York City. Either way, a super volcano with the ability to cause severe long-term damage, maybe even power grid failure, and an active fault line that is predicted to cause well over eighty-six thousand casualties and over three thousand deaths, seems like a fair amount of wrath, especially if these two events occur in or around the same time frame. Just imagining how much the United State would suffer across the board, as a whole nation, is extremely frightening to me.

Luke 21:28 reads, "Now when these things begin

to happen, look up and lift your heads, because your redemption draws near."

Why are all these signs important to us if we believe in Jesus Christ and eternal life through Him? As Christians, one of our largest modern-day concerns is the Second Coming of Christ. During the time it took me to read the entirety of the Bible, it became clear to me that one huge part of my upbringing as a Christian had one fatal flaw regarding the rapture. Are we actually going to be raptured before the tribulation foretold in the book of Revelation as was traditionally taught? Or will we, as believers in Christ, have to go through some perilous and trying times like the rest of the population of nonbelievers? Believe it or not, many people believe that Christians will have to go through some of the, if not the entire, seven-year tribulation leading up to Christ's return. I believe that we will be raptured after the seven-year tribulation; Revelation 7:9-17 supports this belief:

> **After these things I looked, and behold, a great multitude which no one could number, of all nations, tribes, peoples, and tongues, standing before the throne and before the Lamb, clothed with white robes, with palm branches in their hands, and crying out with a loud voice, saying, "Salvation belongs to our God who sits on the throne, and to the Lamb!" All the angels stood around the throne and the elders and the four living creatures, and fell on their faces before the throne and worshiped God, saying:**

> **"Amen! Blessing and glory and wisdom, thanksgiving and honor and power and might, be to our God forever and ever. Amen."**
>
> **Then one of the elders answered, saying to me, "Who are these arrayed in white robes, and where did they come from?"**
>
> **And I said to him, "Sir, you know."**
>
> **So he said to me, "These are the ones who came out of the great tribulation, and washed their robes and made them white in the blood of the Lamb." (Revelation 7:9–17)**

The events of this passage take place just before the seventh seal is opened. In the book of Revelation, the seven seals are opened, then the seven trumpets sound, and then the seven bowls of God's judgment are poured. I believe that the great multitude that no one could number are the Christians who are martyred after the first half of tribulation, after the beast reveals himself.

So, the way I interpret the book of Revelation is this: When the first seal of seven is opened and the Antichrist is put into position, it is the beginning of the first three and a half years of the seven-year tribulation. Immediately after the seventh seal is opened, the angel throws the golden censer filled with fire to the earth and into the sea, and the seven angels prepare to sound their trumpets (Revelation 8:5–6), which is the trigger for the second half. I believe that the time of the seven trumpets is the second half of the seven-year tribulation, also known as the great tribulation that Jesus spoke of in Matthew 24.

Also, as I read the book of Revelation, it appears to me that the events that take place during the opening of the seals intensify and become more rapid. Then the sounding of the trumpets result in events even more intense than the events of the seven seals. By the last trumpet, I believe that the seven bowls of judgment will be poured either almost all at once or very rapidly and successively at the very tail end of the great tribulation. In Matthew 24:22, speaking of the great tribulation, Jesus says, "And unless those days were shortened, no flesh would be saved; but for the elect's sake those days will be shortened." Because of Matthew 24:22, I believe that the rapture will be before the seven bowls of God's judgment are poured. Later on, in Matthew 24:27, Jesus says, "For as the lightning comes from the east and flashes to the west, so also will the coming of the Son of Man be." When will Jesus return? He will return on a white horse after the seven bowls and the finality of Babylon's fall (Revelation 19:11–16).

> **Let no one deceive you by any means; for that Day will not come unless the falling away comes first, and the man of sin is revealed, the son of perdition, who opposes and exalts himself above all that is called God or that is worshiped, so that he sits as God in the temple of God, showing himself that he is God.**

> **Do you not remember that when I was still with you I told you these things? And now you know what is restraining, that he may be revealed in his own time. For the mystery of lawlessness is already at work; only He who now restrains will do so until He is taken out of the way. And then the lawless one will be revealed, whom the Lord will consume with the breath of His mouth and destroy with the brightness of His coming. (2 Thessalonians 2:3–8)**

So the Antichrist will not be revealed until there is a falling away from faith. Many people regard this scripture as proof that the rapture must take place prior to the tribulation. Because of the falling away of faith, God will remove the Holy Spirit, along with all the Christians, which is what restrains the Antichrist from inducing full-on lawlessness upon the earth. However, if you read Daniel 9:27, we find that the Antichrist will break the treaty with Israel and will desecrate God's temple *halfway* through the tribulation. As I interpret this scripture, it seems to me that there is three and a half years' worth of falling away that could take place before the Antichrist breaks his treaty and attempts to set himself up to be worshipped, with God all the while releasing His restraints from the Holy Spirit. I believe that this is the time when the Antichrist reveals himself as the beast, wages war on the two witnesses, and is allowed to kill them along with many followers of Christ (Revelation 11:1-14). Christians and Jews will be hunted down and slaughtered for their faith, much like the Jews in Nazi Germany during the Holocaust—only now the methods and technology will be much more advanced.

> Immediately after the tribulation of those days the sun will be darkened, and the moon will not give its light; the stars will fall from heaven, and the powers of the heavens will be shaken. Then the sign of the Son of Man will appear in heaven, and then all the tribes of the earth will mourn, and they will see the Son of Man coming on the clouds of heaven with power and great glory. And He will send His angels with a great sound of a trumpet, and they will gather together His elect from the four winds, from one end of heaven to the other. (Matthew 24:29-31).
>
> But I do not want you to be ignorant, brethren, concerning those who have fallen asleep, lest you sorrow as others who have no hope. For if we believe that Jesus died and rose again, even so God will bring with Him those who sleep in Jesus.
>
> For this we say to you by the word of the Lord, that we who are alive and remain until the coming of the Lord will by no means precede those who are asleep. For the Lord Himself will descend from heaven with a shout, with the voice of the archangel, and with

> the trumpet of God. And the dead in Christ will rise first. Then we who are alive and remain shall be caught up together with them in the clouds to meet the Lord in the air. And thus we shall always be with the Lord. (1 Thessalonians 4:13-17)

> Now I say, brethren, that flesh and blood cannot inherit the kingdom of God; nor does corruption inherit incorruption. Behold, I tell you a mystery: We shall not all sleep, but we shall all be changed—in a moment, in the twinkling of an eye, at the last trumpet. For the trumpet will sound, and the dead will be raised incorruptible, and we shall be changed. For this corruptible must put on incorruption, and this mortal must put on immortality. So when this corruptible has put on incorruption, and this mortal has put on immortality, then shall be brought to pass the saying that is written: "Death is swallowed up in victory." (1 Corinthians 15:50-54)

As you can see, there are three different scriptures from three different books in the New Testament that have many similarities pointing to a posttribulation rapture. In Matthew 24, after tribulation, Jesus, a.k.a. the Son of man, gathers his elect after the sound of a trumpet. In 1 Thessalonians 4, with the trumpet of God, Jesus arrives, and those who are asleep or dead in Christ rise and are caught up together with the living. In 1 Corinthians 15 we read, "In the twinkling of an eye, at the last trumpet, the dead will be raised and with the living will be changed in order to inherit the kingdom of God during Christ's victory."

After the seventh and last trumpet sounds in Revelation 11, the angels in Revelation 16 begin to pour the bowls of judgment one right after the other. After the last bowl, Christ comes on a white horse (Revelation 19). You may be wondering, *How can Jesus gather His elect after the final bowl of judgment when scripture clearly states that He will descend with the sounding of the trumpet of God?* Remember Matthew 24:27, where Jesus said, "For as the lightning comes from the east and flashes to the west, so also will the coming of the Son of Man be." I believe that in those final moments as judgment is being poured, God is more than capable of gathering His elect in the twinkling of an eye, in a moment, as quick as lightning.

Whether you believe in a pre-, mid-, or post tribulation rapture, I believe that you will agree that it is still important to be ready for emergency situations and the return of Jesus. Undoubtedly there is something going on around us in this world. Also, consider that the Bible describes that there will be birth pains leading up to the actual tribulation, which consists of a period of trying times as well. Jesus says in John 16:33, "These things I have spoken to you, that in Me you may have peace. In the world you will have tribulation; but be of good cheer, I have overcome the world."

3

SURVIVAL PATTERN

The average American person consumes food and water every day. Most people have shelter and are living in a home of some sort. You acquire your food, water, and shelter by paying for them with the money you earn. Not everyone owns a fireplace or has a woodstove in their home; the people who don't use their money to pay the electric or gas bill for heating. When you get in an accident and become injured, you signal emergency medical personnel with your cell phone so that when they arrive, they can provide you with medical aid as first responders on the scene. Most people do not require field craft techniques or prepping to live their day-to-day lives. In the United States, many people don't have the know-how or the capability to defend themselves against a home invasion or a physical attack without calling the police to intervene.

    Everyone is using some form of survival pattern without any real thought or skill involved. The question is, what happens when the unexpected strikes and you no longer have all of these day-to-day commodities available to you? Is it possible that a properly prepared person might not have to struggle through every single part of the pattern for survival? A properly prepared person might have everything needed to survive on hand and may not even require venturing out into the world, not immediately at any rate.

A survival pattern is the things you will need, ranked by level of importance, to survive a certain situation. Included are things that you cannot do without if you want to continue to exist, alive, on this earth, such as food, water, shelter, fire, first aid, and the ability to signal for help. My survival pattern happens to be slightly different from the one suggested by the US military doctrine: prayer, food, water, shelter, fire, first aid, signal/community, and prepping. "Be joyful in hope, patient in affliction, faithful in prayer" (Romans 12:12).

For survival, it is important that you master the individual skills of this pattern so that you become equipped and able to thrive in a survival situation. It is also important to be able to properly develop a pattern for survival based on the situation you may be facing. For me it always begins with prayer. You may be the same way. Do you pray during take-off and landing on a plane trip? Have you ever prayed during a really bad storm while seeking shelter? Or perhaps someone you care about is hurt and in the emergency room because of an injury, and all you can do is pray.

Whether or not you realize this, you are currently in a survival situation in your everyday life, and the dangers could be right in your backyard or just down the street. As civilians living at home in our communities, we have different needs and requirements to survive than do the people serving in the military. If anything, we have more needs. A soldier fighting in foreign lands has his own list of things he will need in order to survive. A US soldier on the battlefield is not burdened with the responsibilities of engaging in combat with his family by his side. This is because the battlefield is in someone else's backyard. Although having a wife and kids or other family members waiting for you back home weighs heavily on the heart of a soldier at war, the soldier's family is not experiencing the same dangers and hardships and, for the most part, are safe and sound.

  I don't care who you are, the number one priority for any parent is providing the best care possible to ensure the survival of your children before your own personal survival. This is a tough job as children are not equipped with the decision-making skills or mental discipline necessary to make it on their own, at least not for the long term. Because of this, parents are required to focus more of, if not most of, their time and energy on monitoring their offspring, as opposed to taking care of just themselves.

> **And not only that, but we also glory in tribulations, knowing that tribulation produces perseverance. (Romans 5:3)**
>
> **My brethren, count it all joy when you fall into various trials, knowing that the testing of your faith produces patience. (James 1:2–3)**

> **Strengthened with all might, according to His glorious power, for all patience and longsuffering with joy. (Colossians 1:11)**

The foregoing are three scriptures in the Bible where survival is translated into perseverance and endurance. Military personnel have health requirements and physical standards they must adhere to in order to perform their jobs effectively. On average, not every American citizen has the same physical abilities as a United States war fighter. Although it is important to set high standards in order to achieve your goals, when dealing with survival, you should also know your limitations; the payoff may not be worth risking your life, a limb, or your eyesight, or that of your loved ones for that matter. Know your limitations by practicing and challenging your skills before they become a requirement to stay alive. The next time you have a cookout in your backyard, build a fire without the use of a lighter. Challenge yourself daily to learn new skills and perform new tasks. Go on that hiking trip in the mountains with your friends or family that you always wanted to take. The more you expose yourself to situations slightly outside your current comfort zone, the more you allow yourself room to grow. You must not limit yourself! In the infantry, we have a saying about training for combat: "Train how you fight, and fight how you train."

"For though we walk in the flesh, we do not war according to the flesh. For the weapons of our warfare are not carnal but mighty in God for pulling down strongholds, casting down arguments and every high thing that exalts itself against the knowledge of God, bringing every thought into captivity to the obedience of Christ, and being ready to punish all disobedience when your obedience is fulfilled" (2 Corinthians 10:3-6).

Just as warfare exists in both the physical world and the spiritual world, so does survival. In the physical world you have to be able to maneuver and execute certain actions in a strategic manner to complete the mission. In order to complete this mission, you may be required to eliminate threats using lethal force. I believe that we need to apply this mentality in the spirit also in the sense that we need to be ruthless.

In physical combat, under most rules of engagement (ROE), soldiers have the right to defend themselves, others, and their equipment. There is a standard for the escalation of force that is emplaced depending on the situation and the mission as it plays out on the battlefield, for example, verbal or visual warning, then warning shots, then lethal force. When you engage the enemy in spiritual warfare, you do not follow the same rules of warfare as in the flesh. Every situation in the spiritual world commands that you terminate the enemy with extreme prejudice, no impunity whatsoever, because that is God's will. And how you do this is by being obedient to God's will and through prayer. While you accomplish obedience through prayer, you can also focus on the physical survival of the physical world.

"Now we exhort you, brethren, warn those who are unruly, comfort the fainthearted, uphold the weak, be patient with all. See that no one renders evil for evil to anyone, but always pursue what is good both for yourselves and for all. Rejoice always, pray without ceasing, in everything give thanks; for this is the will of God in Christ Jesus for you. Do not quench the Spirit. Do not despise prophecies. Test all things; hold fast what is good. Abstain from every form of evil" (1 Thessalonians 5:14-19).

So now that you understand the differences between spiritual survival and physical survival, you may be wondering, *Why then do we need to implement a survival pattern for the end of times? If we are believers in Christ, then shouldn't we be ready to die without fear of death regardless of when the rapture will occur?* I would say yes, that is correct; we shouldn't fear death. However, I believe that in the end times when people are looking for answers and need help and uplifting (just like during the apostle Paul's time in Thessalonica), it will be the Christians who have the foresight to prepare and acquire the skills necessary to survive in the tribulation and who will provide answers from the Word of God. During the end times, it will be our job to harvest souls for God and to be used to save as many people as we can on earth before God's final judgment and the rapture.

So, what if my interpretation of the Bible is wrong and Christians will be raptured before the tribulation period? Then it is all the more urgent to spread the gospel of Christ to as many nonbelievers as we can. Remember, I've already said that we are utilizing a survival pattern right now in our everyday lives. We will go through some trying times before the tribulation. You may be going through trying times right now. If so, take heart; 2 Corinthians 6:2 tells us, "Behold, now is the day of salvation." The time is now to spread the word, harvest souls, and pursue a more meaningful and intimate relationship with God! Don't quench the Spirit, but let the Holy Spirit burn like a blazing fire inside you. Don't look at the end of times as just a terrible time; also see it as a great time because the King of Kings is returning. Do what is right, and do not fall for the tricks of the father of lies and his demons.

"And because lawlessness will abound, the love of many will grow cold. But he who endures to the end shall be saved. And this gospel of the kingdom will be preached in all the world as a witness to all the nations, and then the end will come" (Matthew 24:12–14).

Too many people who are a part of the survival and prepping scene are simply just out for themselves. They already have a mind-set of the flesh that tells them that they will fight their way through anything and kill anyone who gets in their way. These people have a "to each his own" mentality—"everyone for themselves." We've already seen this mentality during natural disasters when people start looting after law-abiding citizens are forced to evacuate their homes and businesses. We've seen this mentality in war-torn countries around the world; some of these places were even considered decent places to visit not too long ago. Even if you could live to be a thousand years old and you are the ultimate survivalist and the last person standing, you're still going to have to die one day—or maybe even miss the boat when Christ returns and then die later anyway. Sooner or later, everyone dies in the flesh, but only the children of God live forever in the Spirit.

"You will be betrayed even by parents and brothers, relatives and friends; and they will put some of you to death. And you will be hated by all for My name's sake. But not a hair of your head shall be lost. By your patience possess your souls" (Luke 21:16–19).

In Luke 21:16–19, Jesus says that it will get so bad that even family members will betray one another and even try to have each other killed. Your friends and your neighbors will hate you because you will claim to be a child of God and believer in Christ. People will worship the Antichrist under the misapprehension that he is the Messiah. Because of this, people will want to persecute you for their own benefit. There will be a system emplaced that will not allow you to buy or sell unless you have the mark of the beast: 666 (Revelation 13). Although it will seem as though Satan is winning and his rule is taking over, his days are short, whereas eternity in heaven with God will last forever. At all costs you will have to resist the mark of the beast and not become part of its system.

"But take heed to yourselves, lest your hearts be weighed down with carousing, drunkenness, and cares of this life, and that Day come on you unexpectedly. For it will come as a snare on all those who dwell on the face of the whole earth. Watch therefore, and pray always that you may be counted worthy to escape all these things that will come to pass, and to stand before the Son of Man" (Luke 21:34–36).

Although you are trying to stay alive and survive in a harsh and dangerous environment, you will need to persevere through prayer and keep watch for the return of the Lord. You will need to keep your eye on the prize, do God's will on earth, and spread the gospel. Praying should be the very first thought during a time of survival before the rest of your survival pattern is carried out. As Colossians 4:2 tells us, "Continue earnestly in prayer, being vigilant in it with thanksgiving."

4

FOOD

Humans cannot survive long without food. At best the average person could go about a week in a survival situation without something to eat. In Ranger School we were fed at least one or two MREs (meals ready to eat) a day, and we still felt like we were dying of starvation. Most Americans eat on average three meals a day, in addition to having the luxury of putting a dollar in a snack machine whenever they feel like it and have a tasty treat appear. In Ranger School we also have that same commodity, only the dollar is invisible. The snack machine is a pine tree, and the tasty treat is a piece of bark. And then you snap out of it and continue your patrol. It's nice being able to have snack machines and MREs, but what happens if it all goes away? Without the ability to live off the land to find food, you will starve to death.

People are capable of doing strange and dangerous things when they are desperate and hungry. I've seen a grown man cry out in agony during Ranger School when he finally had the chance to eat his MRE and, because he lacked dexterity in the moment, his food spilled on the rain-soaked ground in the middle of the night. Of course, that didn't stop him from scooping everything up with his dirty hands, mud included. He dreadfully tried to collect his entrée and ignore the fact that his meal was riddled with dirt. Fatigue had gotten the best of him. He was emotional but didn't care; he just wanted to eat. At first everyone wanted to pretend that it didn't happen so they could just ignore the situation and continue eating their unspoiled meals. But eventually people started to take pity on the soldier and offer their extra creamer and sugar packets, which are usually reserved for the end of the meal as extra last-minute calories. The Ranger School candidate was very appreciative to have received these gifts, and his spirits were lifted almost instantly.

> **When the Son of Man comes in His glory, and all the holy angels with Him, then He will sit on the throne of His glory. All the nations will be gathered before Him, and He will separate them one from another, as a shepherd divides his sheep from the goats. And He will set the sheep on His right hand, but the goats on the left. Then the King will say to those on His right hand, "Come, you blessed of My Father, inherit the kingdom prepared for you from the foundation of the world: for I was hungry and you gave me food; I was thirsty and you gave Me**

> **drink; I was a stranger and you took Me in; I was naked and you clothed Me; I was sick and you visited Me; I was in prison and you came to Me." (Matthew 25:31-36)**
>
> **Then He Said to His disciples, "Therefore I say to you, do not worry about your life, what you will eat; nor about the body, what you will put on. Life is more than food, and the body is more than clothing." (Luke 12:22-23)**

One of the things that helped Ranger School candidates build loyalty within their squad or platoon during the course was sharing any extra food that we were willing to spare, even if it was just a small packet of sugar.

During the end times, one of the things that will separate Christians from other people will be the fact that because we know the Word, we saw the signs, and we are prepared, we will be able to give. I imagine that during the tribulation it would seem more like a common-sense approach to keep to yourself while hoarding your food and keeping it away from others. However, Christians are hidden in Christ (Colossians 3:3). What the Spirit would have you do is to share what you have and use the opportunity to minister to the people who have nothing and are desperately looking for answers. Jesus said that we will be rewarded for doing this by inheriting the kingdom that He has prepared for us.

During these times, people, even other Christians, are likely to turn to Christ and pray for food so that they can feed their families.

Christians who are prepared and equipped to gather food shouldn't worry about taking advantage of the opportunity to be the answer to those prayers, which in turn is the will of God. Remember, Jesus fed five thousand people with just five loaves of bread and two fishes (Luke 9:13–14).

> **And I heard a voice in the midst of the four living creatures saying, "A quart of wheat for a denarius, and three quarts of barley for a denarius; and do not harm the oil and the wine." (Revelation 6:6)**
>
> **He causes all, both small and great, rich and poor, free and slave, to receive a mark on their right hand or on their foreheads, and that no one may buy or sell except one who has the mark or the name of the beast, or the number of his name. Here is wisdom. Let him who has understanding calculate the number of the beast, for it is the number of a man: His number is 666. (Revelation 13:16–18)**

During the tribulation period, the Antichrist will set up his government and will be allowed to rule over a one-world government. There will be a system in place in which no one will be able to buy or sell anything without his mark, the mark of the beast. And as Christians well know, accepting this mark will result in eternal damnation. Furthermore, things will get so bad that a day's wages will only be enough to buy one loaf of bread. The elite of the world under this one-world government will still be able to enjoy the luxuries of oil and wine. Even then, eventually things will get so bad that people won't even care about their money: "They will throw their silver into the streets, and their gold will be like refuse; their silver and their gold will not be able to deliver them" (Ezekiel 7:19).

Because Christians who are not prepared will not be able to feed their families, they will be severely tempted to take the mark of the beast. It is and will be our duty as Christians who are prepared to ensure that our brothers and sisters in Christ are taken care of so that we don't risk losing them to temptation. In those days I believe that unprepared Christians will be filled with doubt, disbelief, and disobedience because of their hunger and desperation. Their faith will be shaken to its core because they were promised a rapture but were not ready to go through tribulation.

> **Then Jesus, being filled with the Holy Spirit, returned from the Jordan and was led by the Spirit into the wilderness, being tempted for forty days by the devil. And in those days He ate nothing, and afterword, when they had ended, He was hungry.**
>
> **And the devil said to Him, "If You are the Son of God, command this stone to become bread."**
>
> **But Jesus answered him, saying, "It is written, 'Man shall not live by bread**

> alone, but by every word of God.'"
> (Luke 4:1-4)

During the tribulation, when the hardship of hunger and the threat of death will be commonplace, it will be absolutely imperative to keep our faith with God. Temptation will be everywhere, and every day will be a struggle. Without the Word of God, Christians will fall victim to the father of lies. Keep in mind that in the foregoing scripture Jesus said "every word of God," so it is extremely important to study now, before we are subjected to a full-blown assault by the devil and all his demons. Thank God for Jesus being able to lead by example and demonstrate a perfect life, resisting the temptation of the devil!

> **Then God said, "Let Us make man in Our image, according to Our likeness; Let them have dominion over the fish of the sea, over the birds of the air, and over the cattle, over all the earth and over every creeping thing that creeps on the earth." (Genesis 1:26)**
>
> **And God said, "See, I have given you every herb that yields seed which is on the face of the earth, and every tree whose fruit yields seed; to you it shall be for food. Also, to every beast of the earth, to every bird of the air, and to everything that creeps on the earth, in which there is life, I have given every green herb for food"; and it was so. (Genesis 1:29-30)**

When God created humankind in the Garden of

Eden, He gave us dominion over the earth and all the living things on the earth. Humankind and all the animals on earth were never designed to be carnivorous and kill and eat one another. At that time everything was in perfect harmony in the Garden of Eden. He created us to be stewards of everything on the earth. So, does that mean we are not supposed to eat animals for survival?

> "Every moving thing that lives shall be food for you. I have given you all things, even as the green herbs. But you shall not eat flesh with its life, that is, its blood" (Genesis 9:3-4).

After the Flood in the book of Genesis, God gave Noah permission for humankind to eat animals and plants, as long as they did not eat the blood. This scripture tells us that blood is the life of the living creature. When Cain killed Abel, Abel's blood cried out to God from the ground after he was dead (Genesis 4:10).

> "For the life of the flesh is in the blood, and I have given it to you upon the altar to make atonement for your souls; for it is the blood that makes atonement for the soul. Therefore I said to the children of Israel, 'No one among you shall eat blood, nor shall any stranger who dwells among you eat blood'" (Leviticus 17:11-12).

Under the old covenant, God commanded Moses that no one was to eat blood because it was reserved for sacrifices for the atonement of sin. However, when Jesus and His disciples took Communion, they drank as a symbol of the blood of Jesus, and a new covenant was formed. In addition, the shedding of Jesus's blood for atonement of our sins was the ultimate, final, once-and-for-all sacrifice so that we could have eternal life in heaven.

Just to be clear, you now know from scripture that you are permitted by God to eat animals and that under the new covenant through Christ, we have no more need of animal blood for sacrifices. Why is this important to you? Because in survival situations in which your life will depend on acquiring food, the chances of successfully gaining calories are few and far between; you will have to use every part of what you harvest in the wild for survival.

There are many ways you can find food in nature outside the modern world. The most common technique is hunting. Your abilities as a hunter, trapper, or fisherman will provide you with enough nutrients to keep moving toward your goals. Food that derives from animals such as deer, squirrels, fish, and even snakes contains the most caloric value per pound.

The variety of ways you can kill an animal in the wild are many and can range from something as primitive as a simple rock on a stick triggered by a string to something as complex as a rifle that costs thousands of dollars. The majority of hunters in the United States hunt for sport and with the aid of a high-powered rifle or shotgun. The use of a rifle is the most prevalent technique in terms of practicality, when available. With the use of a good rifle and accurately set sights, hunting large game is as easy as point, aim, and shoot.

Another popular method of hunting is archery.

Archery hunting can range from bows and arrows to crossbow techniques. As with firearms, there is a wide variety of types and configurations of weapons related to archery hunting. Of all the projectile weapons used for hunting, as it matters in survival, the traditional bow and arrow archery technique is the best method to become proficient in. Apart from spears and bludgeons, the traditional bow and arrow is the oldest method of hunting and is still being used quite frequently today. If you are ever caught in a survival situation and you will need to sustain yourself for a long period of time with no on-hand method of killing, a bow and arrow is simple enough to make and requires less energy than a spear or club to take down your prey. A bow and arrow also will allow you to kill silently, which is quite beneficial when you are trying to survive with possible hostile forces in the area.

How to Make a Bow and Arrow

Initially for your basic field bow all you need is a knife, string, one thick tree limb, and several small branches. I have 550 parachute cord with me at all times. Two ways I constantly carry 550 cord are (1) by wearing a braided bracelet and (2) by replacing my bootlaces with 550 cord. Find a thick branch or a thin log that has a slight bend in it to prevent the bowstring from slamming into your hand. Carve and shape the branch. Make notches on both ends. Ensure that the 550 cord string on both ends is taut. Select straight branches for arrows. Shave the branches and carve the ends, then heat over a fire to shape and harden. As you kill animals, improve your basic bow with bones from large game to make arrowheads and feathers from large birds such as turkey to make your fletching. The best type of wood to use is oak; however, most any type of wood you find in the wilderness will do just fine. Make sure you use healthy wood and not something that looks dry and dead as it will break, resulting in alerted or spooked prey.

For smaller prey such as rabbits, squirrels, and birds, you are better off using a slingshot, which is also easily acquired through the provisions of nature. All species of bird are edible, and their eggs. Some birds will pretend to be injured when you are near their nest if they have eggs. They will wait for you to catch up to them far enough away from the nest and then fly away.

How to Prepare a Bird

The best way to prepare fowl is by plucking the feathers and cooking the bird with its skin still attached. Allowing the skin of your bird to stay intact will afford you more nutrients. Once you have completed the plucking of the bird, cut its head off at the neck as close to the body as you can. You will then have to clean out the insides through the cavity that you have created (just like the Thanksgiving turkey you buy from the store). Ensure that you are washing it out with fresh, clean water. Certain birds may require scalding in order to permit effective plucking of the feathers. Waterfowl such as ducks are best plucked when dry. Be sure to save the neck, liver, and heart to make a stew. Make sure that scavenger-type birds such as buzzards and seagulls are boiled for at least twenty to thirty minutes before cooking in order to kill any retained parasites.

When you are in the wild trying to survive, your own imagination is what sets the limits on your creatively constructing an efficient hunting tool. Traps and snares are effective methods of obtaining food and also are silent, which is useful when you are trying to evade enemy forces. Traps allow you to catch small game while you are in another location stalking larger animals.

Techniques of Trapping

The best trap to use to catch small game such as rabbits and squirrels is a snare. Make a snare simply by using 550 cord strands or thin picture wire to create a slipknot anchored to a tree. Ensure that you place your snare on the animal's trail as most animals will reuse the path that they have previously created. As a rule, you should make the loop of your snare slightly bigger than your prey's head so the shoulders of the animal will get caught and the slipknot will tighten around the animal's neck. Funnel in your game by camouflaging the areas around your snare with extra brush. Picture wire, if available, is your best option as it is harder to chew through. A simple snare attached to a log will suffice; however, a snare run from the tip of a bent-over and sturdy live sapling is more effective. The snare is anchored to the ground using a stake with a notch. Along the snare's line, running halfway between the tip of the tree and its base, is a smaller stick with a counter-notch that will hold the tree in place. This piece is called the trigger. Once the animal becomes ensnared in the trap, the trigger is released and the tree springs upward, causing the animal to struggle more.

To make a proper squirrel snare, tie multiple snares along a single branch leaned up against a tree that appears to have frequent squirrel traffic. Allow some extra length between the anchor on the branch and the actual snare. Use this extra length by twisting picture wire around a thin stick, thus creating a spring that will be able to stand up on its own. This will give the snare a greater chance of randomly snagging the squirrel as it runs up and down the branch. This method is a great technique because you will be able to catch multiple squirrels in the same trap. Squirrels are curious by nature and will be drawn in to investigate the panicked chirps of another squirrel.

More primitive and less effective than the snare is a simple deadfall. To set this trap, use a heavy rock or log that is tilted at a steep angle on top of a figure-four trigger. When an animal goes in for the bait, it will release the trigger, causing the weight to fall and smash down on the prey.

How to Skin Animals

Every type of animal is essentially skinned and dressed the same way. Once you know how to do it, it's relatively easy to do. All you need is a sharp knife. A rope or 550 cord is optional. The main components of dressing and skinning an animal are field dressing, skinning, and sectioning off the animal for meat. After you have killed an animal such as a deer, it is important to clean and dress the carcass as soon as possible. This will make the task easier on you. If you wait too long, the meat and the skin will be harder to separate.

There are several different techniques for

cleaning and dressing an animal. In a survival situation where you may be away from your shelter, it's best to field dress any larger animal such as a deer to allow you to bring your harvest back to camp. The first thing to do is to cut a circle around the anus, ensuring that you do not penetrate too far with your knife. If you cut too deep into any of the digestive parts such as the intestine, bladder, or stomach, you run the risk of contaminating the meat. Once the incision around the anus is complete, pull up and cut around the genitalia while pulling it back toward the anus, cutting along the hip as you cut it loose. Split the pelvis apart with your knife to help spread the legs to provide more room. From the top of the pelvis, cut a hole in the muscle wall and then cut upward, avoiding slicing any guts. Stick two fingers in the hole you have created to pull up space to allow room for your knife, and slice all the way toward the sternum. Split through the rib cage all the way to the throat, and cut loose the esophagus and trachea. Starting from the top, pull out all the guts, making sure you split the pelvic bone first. As you are pulling all the entrails out, cut the diaphragm loose.

Once all the entrails are out, turn the animal over so the opening faces down. This will allow the blood to drain. If you are able, collect the blood as it will serve as a valuable source of food and salt after boiled.

Now that the entrails have been removed and the blood has been drained, the animal weighs much less and is easier to transport back to camp. When you are ready to skin the animal, it is oftentimes easier to hang the animal upside down from a convenient limb to assist with the process. Hang larger animals by the tendons of the hind legs. If you are unable to hang the animal, it's okay to lay animal flat on its back as when it was field dressed. Once you are ready, cut rings around the front and hind legs just behind the joints. Skin the animal by going under the skin with your knife and slicing up the inside the legs. Next, peel all the skin down, keeping every part of the hide intact. Once the skin has been pulled all the way down past the meaty part of the neck toward the head, cut a ring all the way around the neck, which will allow you to remove the skin completely. Keep in mind that you are able to eat the meaty parts of the head such as the eyes, tongue, and brain.

The last thing you want to do is to section off all the meat to ensure that you are able to consume as much as the animal as possible. Quarter the animal. Remove the front quarters by cutting around the shoulders, and remove the hindquarters by cutting around the hips. Next, cut the back straps from each side of the spine. Any meat left in or around the ribs is also edible.

Skinning small game such as a squirrel is as easy as creating a slit across the back about midway. Insert your index and middle fingers from both hands into the opening, and pull in opposite directions. The skin will peel off with ease.

Any animal bones large enough can be carved into the shape of an arrowhead or other types of tools.

Don't rule out a sturdy stick sharpened to a point as a good tool for hunting. Such a tool will serve you well as a backup weapon should your original weapon fail to be as effective as originally thought. A solid stick is a great device for clubbing snakes when encountered at random. All poisonous and nonpoisonous freshwater and land snakes are edible.

How to Skin a Snake

The first thing you want to do is to cut off the snake's head. Make sure that you bury the head in the ground so no one will accidentally step on the snake's fangs and become poisoned even though the snake is dead. Next, make a slit and cut open the snake's belly in order to remove its innards. Snake guts are good for luring in animals for traps and can be used as fishing bait as well. The final step in preparing a snake for food is peeling off the skin.

How to Prepare and Cook Fish

Knowing how to effectively catch fish is an invaluable skill. Fishing can be as simple as putting a hook on a piece of string and applying some bait to the end of the hook before placing it in the water. There is a plethora of ways you can catch fish. Use the smaller inside strands known as "the guts" of any 550 cord tied together to make fishing lines, nets, and cages.

All freshwater fish are edible. You must, however, ensure that you properly prepare the fish and cook it thoroughly to kill any parasites that may coexist in its water source.

As soon as you catch a fish, cut out the gills and the large blood vessels all along the backbone. To prevent your fish from spoiling, it is important to immediately cut out the gills. Next, scale the fish by shaving off any scales with a sharp knife. Gut the fish by cutting open its stomach and scraping it clean. Do this by sticking your knife in the fish's anus and cutting upward through the belly. Then remove the entrails. If the fish has no scales, you will need to skin it. Smaller fish less than four inches in length do not require gutting but should still be skinned and scaled. You should also cut the fish's head off unless you are going to cook it on a stick. You can use the nonedible parts of any fish you catch as bait for catching more fish. You can also use the small pointy bones of previously caught fish or animals you have trapped as an improvised hook. In addition, it is possible to use carved-out pieces of wood to make a hook. Your imagination is the limit. Use whatever you can find, for example, safety pins and paper clips.

After wild animals, your next best option for consuming nutrients is to eat insects. John the Baptist, for example, survived on wild honey and locusts. Insects can be found virtually anywhere plants and animals are found. Most insects can be eaten raw, with the exception of beetles and grasshoppers, which are best served by taking off their wings and legs and then cooking them to destroy any parasites. A good way to prepare a large collection of insects is to grind them all into a paste for an easier, more filling meal. This paste can be combined with smashed-up edible plants and can be consumed either cooked or raw.

Along with insects, you have the option to consume worms. Worms should be prepared by putting them in a container of clean water for a few minutes to allow them to purge themselves naturally. When you are collecting worms, put wet grass, moss, or mud in the container with them so they do not dehydrate. Another source of food provided by nature apart from animals and insects is plants, fruits, and vegetables. Although foraging for edible plants is not as reliable as hunting animals, it is still an option. Different areas of the United States have several types of indigenous edible plants, vegetables, and fruits. A survivor's best option is to stick with the more commercial types of fruits and vegetables that you would normally see in a grocery store or grow in your own garden, such as corn, pumpkins, apples, and blueberries. Know your area, study the more common types of plants that are plentiful, and dedicate your time to foraging for those types. In a desert environment you can count on being able to eat and drink from cactus plants. In a heavily forested area there are several types of acorns that all can be eaten either raw or boiled. During the winter months, green pine needles can be found under snow and crushed, boiled, and filtered to make a lifesaving tea with good vitamins. Ripe tropical fruits such as oranges should be eaten raw.

It is important that you be able to recognize the different types of plants in the wilderness, both edible and poisonous. Tasting or ingesting even the smallest amount of a nonedible plant can make you extremely sick, resulting in discomfort and, at worst, death. While in a survival situation, if you require food and you come across a questionable plant that you cannot positively identify but still intend on eating, apply the universal edibility test. This test requires over twenty-four hours to ensure you will not be poisoned, so make sure that eating this plant is worth your time and energy. Each part of the plant that you intend on eating will need to be tested. Also make sure there is enough of that type of plant to provide the nutrients you require. If not, then you should move on.

Ensure that you eat only one part of any suspect plant at a time. If you eat a large amount of plant food on an empty stomach, you may develop diarrhea, nausea, or painful cramps. These symptoms can occur even after eating food you know to be safe to eat, such as apples, wild onions, acorns, and dandelions.

Before even using the universal edibility method, be sure to reject certain plants right away. Potentially poisonous plants show these characteristics:

- milky sap (besides dandelions)
- spines, fine hairs, and thorns (besides prickly pear, thistles, and bracken fern fiddleheads)
- mushrooms and fungi nearby
- umbrella-shaped flowers
- bulbs (besides onions, which are easily identified by their distinct smell)
- grain heads with pink, purplish, or black spurs
- beans or seeds inside pods
- old or wilted leaves
- shiny leaves
- white or yellow berries
- an almond scent to the woody parts and leaves.

Once you have found a questionable plant that you wish to eat, and if it does not have any of the characteristics of potentially poisonous or toxic plants, you should apply the universal edibility test for plants, which is something I was taught way back when I was a Cub Scout:

- Refrain from eating eight hours prior to the test, and drink only purified water.
- During the eight-hour period of abstaining from food, test for contact poisoning by placing a piece of the plant on the inside of your elbow or wrist. The sap or juice should contact the skin. Usually fifteen minutes is enough time for a reaction to develop.
- Test only one part of the plant at a time.
- Separate the plant into its basic components—stems, roots, bulbs, and flowers.
- Smell the food for strong acrid odors. (Fragrance alone does not indicate whether or not a plant is edible.)
- During testing, take nothing by mouth except purified water and the plant that you are testing.
- Select a small portion of a single part of the plant, and prepare it in the way that you intend on eating it.
- Before placing the prepared plant in your mouth, touch a small portion (a pinch) to the outer surface of your lip to test for burning or itching.
- If after three minutes there is no reaction on your lip, place the plant on your tongue, and hold it there for fifteen minutes.
- If there is no reaction, thoroughly chew a pinch and hold it in your mouth for fifteen minutes. Do not swallow. If any ill effects occur, rinse out your mouth with purified water.

- ▶ If nothing abnormal occurs, swallow the food and wait eight hours. If any ill effects occur during this period, induce vomiting and drink a water and charcoal mixture.
- ▶ If no effects occur, eat one-quarter cup of the same plant prepared the same way. Wait another eight hours. If no ill effects occur, then you know that the plant part as prepared is safe for eating.

Once you have found a good, usable plant for a food source, it is important that you prepare and eat the plant correctly to avoid getting sick. Cook any underground portions you intend to eat, if possible, to eliminate any possible bacterial contamination. You most likely won't know what substances have been used in the ground to provide nutrition for the vegetation you are eating. In Third World countries like Afghanistan, it is not uncommon for crops to be grown with human fecal matter mixed in with the rest of the manure. Also, cooking these types of root plants and vegetables will aid in digestion as they will most likely have high starch levels. If you find yourself in an evasion type of situation, you will want to avoid creating fires, thus limiting yourself to mainly leafy green vegetables and aboveground plants and fruits. Ripe tropical fruits such as oranges and bananas should be peeled and eaten raw.

5

WATER

Just like with food, humans cannot survive without water. In fact, without water, the food you have procured while trying to survive will be rendered useless. The average person cannot go without this necessity for more than three days and still be able to function properly for survival. The average person requires at least three liters of water a day to self-sustain. Three liters is not much when you are in a survival situation, sweating and working harder than you normally would because you are trying to achieve your goals for your survival pattern.

During patrols in Ranger School, one of the things that I found most comforting was that I could drink whatever water was available to me whenever I got thirsty. Although we were lacking in sleep and food, we seemed to always have water. A large reason for this was that the instructors were responsible for our safety and made sure that we acquired water regularly. It would have been impossible to carry on and conduct training without water. Without water, instead of learning how to be rangers, we would have been in a constant struggle for survival.

> **The Lord will guide you continually,**
>
> **And satisfy your soul in drought,**
>
> **And strengthen your bones;**
>
> **You shall be like a watered garden,**
>
> **And like a spring of water, whose waters do not fail.**
>
> **—Isaiah 58:11**

If you are ever struggling to survive, or if you are on the run, fatigued, and thirsty, remember that God is always with you. No matter what you are facing, God will lead you to where you need to be. When you feel like giving up, that is when God will strengthen you the most. With God, anything is possible without fail. When you face adversity and you remember that God wants you to survive, you will literally be like a thriving, watered garden.

> "I indeed baptize you with water unto repentance, but He who is coming after me is mightier than I, whose sandals I am not worthy to carry. He will baptize you with the Holy Spirit and fire" (Matthew 3:11).

The water that is used for baptism is a symbol of a person's repentance. We are cleansed because

Jesus washes away our sins. During the end times leading up to God's final judgment, people are going to run either toward God or away from Him. When you run toward God and become a follower of Christ, you repent and then are filled with the Holy Spirit. God's final judgment before He brings His kingdom on earth will be to cast those who do not repent into the lake of fire.

"He who receives you receives Me, and he who receives Me receives Him who sent Me. He who receives a prophet in the name of a prophet shall receive a prophet's reward. And he who receives a righteous man in the name of the righteous man shall receive a righteous man's reward. And whoever gives one of these little ones only a cup of cold water in the name of a disciple, assuredly, I say to you, he shall by no means lose his reward" (Matthew 10:40–42).

When we become followers of Jesus, we become one of His disciples. So when our brothers and sisters in Christ are thirsty, we are required to give them water. When we receive these disciples as guests and treat them accordingly, we stand to receive our heavenly reward, which God has promised us. If you are indeed a follower of Christ, you will love God with all your heart and love your neighbor as you love yourself.

> "He who believes in Me, as the Scripture said, 'From his innermost being will flow rivers of living water'" (John 7:38).

Water is such an essential part of life that when you believe in and accept Jesus and His sacrifice for the whole world, living water will flow inside you for all eternity. Rivers often lead through parts of terrain that suddenly drop off into waterfalls. As the river gets closer to the waterfall, it increases in speed and its current crashes against the rocks along the way, forming rapids. During the end times when things get rocky and you reach drop-offs, you will need the living waters of Christ flowing through you like the powerful roaring rapids that they are.

> **Jesus answered and said to her, "If you knew the gift of God, and who it is who says to you, 'Give Me a drink,' you would have asked Him, and He would have given you living water."**
>
> **The woman said to Him, "Sir, You have nothing to draw with, and the well is deep. Where then do You get that living water? Are You greater than our father Jacob, who gave us the well, and drank from it himself, as well as his sons and his livestock?"**
>
> **Jesus answered and said to her, "Whoever drinks of this water will thirst again, but whoever drinks of the water that I shall give him will never thirst. But the water that I shall give him will become in him a fountain of water springing up into everlasting life." (John 4:10–15)**

Throughout the Bible, the Word of God uses water to symbolize faith, salvation, and delivery. Water is essential to staying alive; Jesus is essential to everlasting life in heaven. When you war in the flesh, you run the risk of eventually being physically harmed or even getting killed in battle. When you war in the spirit, defeat is not even an option because Christ has already healed us and defeated death.

When you war in the flesh and war in the spirit, think of your physical thirst. When you drink water to survive physically, you eventually become again thirsty and need more. The less water you consume, the higher risk you have of becoming dehydrated and facing the possibility of death. The living water that Jesus gives you in the spirit quenches your thirst forever.

When you do have water, make sure that you do not let it go to waste by not drinking it and storing it for later. When you do drink your water, it's best to take small sips rather than gulping it down quickly. If you drink it too fast, your body will not have enough time to absorb it, and you will pass it as urine. Every bodily function is only made possible with the use of water. Keep in mind that if the survival situation you happen to be in includes the possibility of running into hostile forces, those who may be pursuing you are also seeking natural water sources.

When I went through basic training for the US Army, the drill sergeants made sure that each individual was consuming at least eight liters of water a day. All privates going through the training were required to carry a single strand of 550 cord, girth-hitched through the buttonhole on their collar. As the day went on, we were required to tie a knot in the cord for every liter of water consumed. Should a trainee fall short of the requirement at the end of the day, forced hydration would be induced.

It's hard to believe that people tend to stay

hydrated by surviving off sodas without any pure water at all. When I was a kid, you couldn't give me enough water; I used to even drink it straight from the hose. While trying to survive, do not drink urine, fish juices, blood, seawater, alcohol, or recently frozen ice from the sea. Although sodas are not the worst thing in the world to drink, it is still best to stick with water. Just because you are not in a survival-type situation doesn't mean that you couldn't be in an instant. Always keep hydrated. If you get thirsty, it's too late; you are already dehydrated. You should begin drinking water immediately. If your urine is yellow, you are becoming dehydrated and in need of water. If your urine is orange or even a light brownish color, you are dehydrated and overworked, or you may have a urinary tract infection. You need to ensure that you drink water at all times.

Many people suggest that drinking your own urine in a survival-type situation is a good way to stay hydrated. Drinking your own urine to survive is possible; however, your urine contains salt, which has the potential to dehydrate you, much like salt water. It is important that any urine you intend on drinking is distilled and filtered. Keep in mind that the volume of urine you expel will decrease each time you filter it through your body after you drink it. It is imperative to continue searching for water even if you are able to distill and filter your urine and drink it.

There are many other things that water can provide for you besides hydration. Humans need water to keep clean in order to maintain proper hygiene. Using water to clean a wound will help prevent infections when injured. Water also affords people the ability to keep cool when it is hot outside.

There are several different types of water sources that the world has to offer: surface water, precipitation, subsurface water, and groundwater.

The most basic way to obtain water in a survival-type situation is to collect it from surface water or from lakes, springs, rivers, and/or streams. The planet is made up of 75 percent water. Most of it is salt water from the oceans and the seas, which is undrinkable unless properly dealt with. Many of the freshwater sources in the United States located in or near urban areas are polluted with human waste and cannot be safely consumed unless the water is suitably treated.

The water in the rural parts of the United States has a greater chance of not being tainted and therefore is more suitable for consumption. It is important to remember that a water source far away from civilization still may house parasites. When surviving in the wild, you want to avoid drinking water from stagnant pools that appear to have an algae population. Also, drinking water downstream from a dead, rotting carcass puts you at high risk of consuming pollutants. Looking out for these types of hazardous indications will better enable you to select a good site for collecting your drinking water.

You may also gather water from precipitation such as rain and snow. As long as you have a clean container, you will be able to drink water that is collected from rainfall. After ensuring certain plants are nonpoisonous, a good way of collecting rainwater would be to use the leaves of trees and plants. When it starts raining, look for a leaning tree and wrap some cloth around its base with a small tail hanging. Underneath the hanging tail, have your clean container ready to collect. While on the move, absorbent cloth wrapped around your ankles will allow you to collect dew from tall grass. Once you are able to wring out the cloth into a container, you should purify the water collected.

Melted snow is a good option for collecting water in cold winter environments. All you need is a clean container that won't melt over a fire. Keep in mind that you do not want to eat ice or snow as a source of water. Eating ice or snow will lower your body temperature and can actually dehydrate you. In addition, ice and snow can cause cold weather injuries to your mouth.

Subsurface water sources require that you dig for your water. Wells and cisterns are considered to be subsurface water sources. If you are able to maintain a static position in the wild, digging a water still is a very effective way of collecting your water.

How to Dig a Water Still:

- ▶ Dig a hole in the ground.
- ▶ Place a container in the center of the hole.
- ▶ Surround the container with moisture producers such as plants and mud.
- ▶ Place a clear plastic sheet over the hole.
- ▶ Anchor the plastic around the edges of the hole with rocks.

- ▶ Place a rock in middle of the plastic sheet over the container as a weight, allowing the plastic to sag slightly.
- ▶ Moisture will condense and run down into the container of the anchor point above it.

How to Find Water in the Desert

Create your own cistern by digging a hole in the ground. Place as much of your waterproof poncho or tarp as you can in the hole, pushed up against the flat bottom and sides of the hole to form a lining. Anchor the excess portions of the tarp to the ground outside the hole with rocks. Ensure that you cover this reservoir when not in use so as not to lose your collected water to evaporation. When it begins to rain, uncover the hole to collect the rainwater. Make sure you watch out for any breeding mosquitoes in your makeshift cistern, and purify the water before drinking and bathing. This method is, after all, creating your own stagnant water source.

If there are no surface or subsurface water sources available and precipitation looks unlikely, you will want to begin searching for groundwater sources. This type of water source is the hardest to acquire and takes a fair amount of skill. Look for groundwater by searching for lush green vegetation. Plants need water just like any other living thing.

Another useful technique is to extract water from plants by means of evaporation. Nonpoisonous plants can be placed in a clear plastic bag and water can be extracted with the use of the sun or some other heat source such as fire. When the sun heats up the plants in the bag, water will begin to evaporate from the plant. As the water vapors reach the barrier of the bag, the process of condensation will begin. Place the plastic bag against a sloped or leaning object so as the water starts to build up, it will collect toward the bottom of the bag. The water in the bag can be purified to drink.

When water is scarce, keep in mind that animals seen in the wild are good indicators of groundwater. Birds will fly toward a water source in the early morning or late afternoon, where they will feed and roost. Different species of animals will share the same water source. Look for intersecting trails that become one, usually in the shape of a *V*, as these often lead toward water holes. If you are pestered by swarming insects, this is more than likely a good sign that there are low drainage points nearby.

There are many different techniques you can use to ensure that the water you have collected for survival purposes will not get you sick. Typically, water procured from plants does not require treatment. I still consider it practical to purify water from plants if you have the time to do so. If you do not, then exercise caution and properly decontaminate the water you intend to drink or use for washing your eating utensils and dishes. When drinking water that isn't decontaminated, you run a great risk of consuming parasites that will give you diarrhea. Diarrhea diminishes the motivation you require to continue to survive. Diarrhea is uncomfortable, often painful, and potentially life-threatening as it means you have to work extra hard to find a good, clean source of drinking water so as to remain properly hydrated.

One of the simplest and most frequently used methods of decontaminating drinking water is to boil the water for a minimum of one minute to eliminate parasites. I personally recommend boiling your drinking water for ten minutes.

Another basic way to ensure that you have drinkable water is to use purifications drops. As a rule, use eight drops of 2.5 percent iodine solution per quart of water. This is the method that was used most frequently when I was going through the Ranger School course. Water was collected from moving rivers, and one ranger candidate would collect all the one-quart canteens and apply the purification drops. Make sure that once the drops have been added, the water stands for at least ten minutes before being consumed. This is a sensible method when you are constantly on the move and seek to avoid detection and capture as you will be able to continue moving while waiting for the ten minutes to pass.

Another effective way of purifying water is to use tablets instead of drops. We seldom used this method in Ranger School. Drinking water tablets are intended for short-term survival use only. The water tablets are made up of an iodine-based compound that usually contains no chlorine. Once the container of tablets is opened, it is best to discard it after a year has passed. After a year has passed, the effects of the tablets decrease, and the chances of accidentally drinking contaminated water increase. The water you treat with tablets should be allowed to sit for thirty minutes before being consumed. Always be sure to read the instructions before using tablets to purify drinking water.

Creating your own filter in a survival situation

is a very effective way of purifying water if you do not have purification drops or tablets. I still recommend boiling the water after it has been filtered, just because you don't know what kind of contaminants are contained in the materials used to construct the filter. The type of filter you can make in the wild will use coarse gravel, fine gravel, coarse sand, charcoal fragments, and/or fine sand. You also need some form of container such as an empty two-liter soda bottle and a small piece of fabric or cloth.

How to Make a Water Filter:

- Cut the bottom of the two-liter bottle, creating a large opening.
- Turn the bottle upside down, and unscrew the cap.
- Replace the cap with cloth or fabric stretched over the small opening and tied tightly.
- Fill the bottle from its larger opening with fine sand first, then charcoal fragments, coarse sand, and fine gravel, with coarse gravel on top.
- Place a clean container underneath the smaller opening with fabric.
- Pour water into the larger opening.
- As water filters through and drains out the smaller opening with the stretched fabric, collect the filtered water in the clean container.

6

SHELTER

After a hard day's work at the office, you return home, possibly to a nice home-cooked meal. After dinner, you allow your chow to digest while you sit back and recline and watch your favorite television program. As it starts to get late, you continue to decompress the events of your day by stepping into a nice steaming hot shower. As you run your fingers through your hair, you allow the water to filter in and out of your mouth and through your teeth. It feels nice to be clean as you dry off.

You are wearing clean nightclothes as you brush your teeth and down a small cup of water. After you say your prayers, you begin to enjoy a good night's sleep. You awake refreshed and ready to perform a whole new series of events during your workday. As you exit your driveway, you glance at your house in the rearview mirror, totally appreciating the sanctuary you will have waiting for you at the end of the day when you return home again.

In a perfect world, you appreciate your job and are truly happy with the things you do for work. You eat healthy and are able to shake off all your work-induced stress before enjoying a full eight hours of uninterrupted, peaceful sleep. Of course, anyone who is reading this can attest that we most certainly do not live in a perfect world. If you have kids, you are most likely not getting the proper amount of sleep to function as a sane human being. Most people do, however, have a warm place called home to eat, bathe, and sleep in.

Your home is your shelter in which you and your family are protected from the elements. Your home is where you make preparations for the next day. Most people are inclined to maintain their homes in good operable condition. Any damage that occurs to your castle is usually dealt with immediately to reduce the risk of further destruction. On the weekends you mow your lawn during the warm months of the year to keep unwanted insect activity at bay. All the while, you are beautifying your landscape and keeping it in a neat, orderly fashion.

If there is one thing that we can count on throughout the Bible, it is that God's plan often places His people in the wilderness. Moses led the Israelites through the wilderness for forty years (Exodus 16:35). John the Baptist was in the wilderness when the Word of God came to him to preach baptism and repentance (Luke 3:2–3). Jesus went into the wilderness to fast when He was tempted by Satan (Matthew 4:1). Why would it be any different for us during the prophesied days of tribulation?

While surviving in the wilderness either as

an individual or as a ranger platoon on patrol, the same concept of home applies to your shelter or security perimeter. Only now your preparations that make you able to perform the next day's tasks are called "patrol base operations," and you complete these in a special sequence called "priorities of work."

> "The Lord repay your work, and a full reward be given you by the Lord God of Israel, under whose wings you have come for refuge." (Ruth 2:12).

God has promised us a full, everlasting reward in heaven for doing His will on earth. Because we are children of God, we will always have a home in His kingdom. God is also our protector who sent His only Son to die for our sins.

> "And if it seems evil to you to serve the Lord, choose for yourselves this day whom you will serve, whether the gods which your fathers served that were on the other side of the River, or the gods of the Amorites, in whose land you dwell. But as for me and my house, we will serve the Lord" (Joshua 24:15).

Everyone is given the free will to choose to serve the Lord. If you do not worship God, then you have chosen to serve the devil. There is no in-between. If it does not glorify God and it's not His will, then it is for evil. God hates evil. As Christians, we need to be very clear and let it be known that Satan and his demons are absolutely not welcome in our homes.

> **Because you have made the Lord, who is my refuge,**
>
> **Even the Most High, your dwelling place,**
>
> **No evil shall befall you,**
>
> **Nor shall any plague come near your dwelling;**
>
> **For He shall give His angels charge over you,**
>
> **To keep you in all your ways.**
>
> **In their hands they shall bear you up,**
>
> **Lest you dash your foot against a stone.**
>
> **You shall tread upon the lion and the cobra,**
>
> **The young lion and the serpent you shall trample underfoot.**
>
> —Psalm 91:9-13

As believers in Christ, we have made our spiritual dwelling place in God. Because of your value to God, Satan wants you to be destroyed. However, God is infinitely more powerful than Satan. Even the angels whom God gave charge to watch over us are infinitely more powerful than demons. Because of this, no plague or evil thing will inhabit your dwelling, because God's angels are constantly fighting a spiritual battle on your bealf.

> **Look at the birds of the air, for they neither sow nor reap nor gather into barns; yet your heavenly Father feeds them. Are you not of more value than they? (Matthew 6:26)**
>
> **Cast your burden on the Lord,**
> **And He shall sustain you;**
> **He shall never permit the righteous**
> **to be moved.**
>
> **—Psalm 55:22**

God loves you so much that He does not want you to worry. At the end of the day, whatever we are going through in this world, whether it involves our job or our relationships, or if we're struggling to survive, it is all in God's hands. His plan is perfect.

When you are in survival mode and are working hard to find shelter, remember that God will sustain you. As Christians, we are made righteous because of our faith in Christ's ultimate sacrifice (Romans 3:22). God will plant your feet on solid ground so that you will not be moved (Psalm 40:2). Thank God that He places such great value on us!

> **The Lord will also roar from Zion,**
> **And utter His voice from Jerusalem;**
> **The heavens and the earth will shake;**
> **But the Lord will be a shelter for His people,**
> **And the strength of the children of Israel.**
>
> **—Joel 3:16**

During the end of the age, God will bring destruction and judgment upon the earth. The world will be flooded with the presence of the supernatural, on both sides. Jesus told us in 24 in the book of Matthew that even the Antichrist will perform miracles to try to fool people. But God is the ultimate victor, whose roar is so powerful that it will shake heaven and earth, not just a little bit but so massively that the whole world will have no choice but to recognize that it is the action of the one true God. Thank God that in all this awesome show of force on the earth leading to His final judgment, He still has love enough for His children to provide them with shelter and strength. It's our job not to let these heavenly provisions go to waste and to obediently carry out His will.

When you are on your own in the wilderness, your first level of physical protection is some sort of shelter. Once you have constructed your accommodation, you become open for business to stay dry and warm. Should you fail to possess a type of shelter while trying to stay alive, you open yourself up to exposure to the elements, which could potentially become hazardous to your health.

When you are exposed and have a low level of comfort, you also lose a considerable amount of sleep. All humans require at least four hours of sleep in order to properly function. With continuous sleep deprivation, your immune system will diminish significantly. Sleep deprivation reduces a person's ability to make sensible decisions or do the simplest of tasks. Your mental status plays a huge role in your survival. When you are trying to survive with the bare minimum, each decision you make is extremely important and may mark the tipping point between life and death. This is one of the reasons that in Ranger School your sleep while on patrol is severely limited. It's a good way to induce stress that simulates the real-life stress of combat, which in turn allows the ranger to catch a glimpse of what a soldier's integrity and leadership skills look like under pressure and amid the decision-making process.

The first thing that comes to mind when the average person considers shelter in the wilderness is a tent or maybe even a log cabin. Tents are very common and are easily obtainable from many stores. Tents that you buy from a store vary considerably in price and in quality. Some things to take into account are the trade-offs between weight and size. You don't have to have the greatest, most state-of-the-art tent to live comfortably when roughing it in the brush. A simple tarp or poncho with a bit of string or rope can provide you with the same necessities that any high-end tent affords.

These are the special considerations that apply when you are determining which type of shelter you will need to survive:

- ▶ Evasion
- ▶ Food and water supply
- ▶ Natural hazards to be avoided—dead standing trees, drainage areas, and susceptibility to flash floods and/or avalanches, etc.
- ▶ Protection from wind and rain with minimal improvements required

- Reflectivity for a heat source as well as ventilation
- Materials needed for building

If there is a potential that enemy forces will be present, do not occupy the area for more than twenty-four hours. When selecting an area in which to construct a shelter, choose terrain that any hostile forces would not want to use for any tactical purposes, and avoid any known or suspected hostile locations. Avoid any built-up areas with natural lines of drift. Be wary of ridges, hilltops, and valleys. Also stay away from any footpaths or roads.

If you do want to be found and there are no potential hostiles in the area, these are characteristics that you would normally welcome. Your best chance to be found is to build your shelter on a hilltop with very few trees and vegetation. Your fire and your signals can be easily identified from a greater distance. Either way, enemies or not, your shelter should be near a water source but not right next to one.

How to Make a Lean-To

A poncho can supply most of what it takes to create an ideal survival shelter called a lean-to. This is the most common type of survival shelter and is also the easiest to construct. I carry a military-type GI poncho and even some bungee cords every time I go into the woods, even if just for one day of hunting.

- Find two trees a little more than a body's length apart.
- Tie a single rope taut between the two trees.

- Drape one of the long ends of the poncho over the rope, and secure.
- Stake the other side to the ground at a forty-five-degree angle using makeshift stakes from sticks.
- Build a wall of sticks and logs on the open side to reflect heat from a fire and also to aid in shielding you from the elements, keeping in mind that a fire too close to the poncho will melt the waterproof material.
- Use dry pine needles and leaves to make bedding to reduce loss of body heat through the ground, keeping in mind that dry leaves and pine needles are extremely flammable and often house ticks.

A lean-to shelter is still an option without a poncho at your disposal. Only now you must lean multiple branches at a forty-five-degree angle instead of draping a poncho over two limbs. Additional branches may be intertwined for more suitable overhead waterproofing. Combining both the poncho and the field-expedient lean-to methods is the best option for optimal protection from the elements.

Keeping off the ground is a great way to conserve body heat and prevent it from being absorbed into the ground. In addition, staying off the ground will help you stay dry. One of the best ways that I've used to do this is to build a hammock. Use the same two trees as you used for the lean-to. Now take a poncho liner and wrap both ends with 550 cord. Ensure that you have enough excess cord to wrap the tail ends around the trees before tying them off. Next, tie a single strand of paracord to both trees. As you did for the lean-to, drape your poncho over the cord, only this time do it at the halfway point. Use two sticks of equal length to brace the two corners at both ends, creating an A-frame roof over your hammock. Make sure not to hang your hammock too high, as you will find it difficult to reach any gear you may stow beneath you on the ground. Also, if you are too high up, you may find yourself in an undesirable position should you become alerted and are forced to react to a situation in the darkness of night. Using a hammock was one of my favorite go-to methods for sleeping out in the field while in the army.

Creating a platform with logs and branches is another method to keep your body off the ground. Use three large branches lashed together into a triangle as a base. Use smaller branches laid across in rows to create solid raft-like flooring. If trees are available, create the triangle to fit between trees. Tie the triangle to the trees at about knee height to create even more space between your body and the ground. Create a second, smaller pallet to place underneath for any gear you wish to keep dry by using the same A-frame poncho roof as in the hammock method. Instead of smaller branches, tie a poncho liner to the triangle to provide a good platform when tied to trees at knee height.

Building a Bunker

There are other situations for which you may want to take the opposite approach of keeping off the ground. Instead, build your shelter in the ground, creating a bunker or hastily constructed fighting position when you are pursued by enemy or hostile forces. The best bunkers are dug in as deep as chest level to provide a better position for shooting a firearm from when needed. If you do not have enough time to dig a complete bunker, dig about a foot and a half deep that will suffice as temporary fighting position before you have to move out. When you are digging out your bunker position, save the topsoil and keep the rest of the dirt or sand separate.

Determine on which side of your bunker the opening for entering and exiting will be. At the opening of your bunker, cut out a slope that will taper into the ground. This slope should only be a little more than shoulder length.

At the entrance, place two sturdy stakes cut from thick branches. The two stakes should only be a foot in length and stick out of the ground. Once your hole is completely dug out and the stakes are in place, create the same type of pallet you would use for building an off-the-ground platform. Place the pallet on top of the two stakes at the entrance, and lash it to the stakes to create a stable rooftop. Reinforce the sides and top of the roof with the dirt from the hole. The dirt will provide ballistic protection from most projectiles and will aid in preventing overhead water leaks. Most traditional military bunkers are reinforced by filling sandbags with the dirt from a hole. Now that the dirt is in place, put the remaining topsoil over the dirt to provide a more natural look with the intent of blending your bunker in with the surrounding area. You may also apply fresh branches to further break up the outline of your bunker. In addition, creating a pallet for the inside flooring and the walls will help keep the inside dry if flooded and keep the walls from caving in. The time and energy required to create a shelter as strong and durable as a bunker is best invested if you intend on surviving at that specific location for a long duration of time.

Fallen Trees

Provided by nature, fallen trees may provide the foundation for a lean-to. Most of the framework for the slanted rooftop is already constructed. If the tree is still fresh, the green leaves or needles will provide camouflage depending on which season it is. Ensure that the base of the tree that rests on the top of the stump is stable and will not fall on top of you. It's best to ensure stability by tying the fallen tree to its own stump. Next, take a knife or hatchet and chop away at the inside branches of your A-frame, creating a hollowed-out space to live in. Use the extra branches that you have just acquired to fill in any gaps between the branches that are still intact. Depending on your situation, you may want to consider giving this particular shelter a more natural look to better conceal your position. Use rope or 550 guts to tie it off wherever necessary.

Caves

Solid rock structures such as caves can provide good shelter. Most of the heavy lifting is already done. Make sure that your cave is not too deep and is in stable-looking condition with no stalactites. Caves are dangerous to clear because you don't know what type of potentially dangerous animals may have inhabited the cave before you, such as bears, snakes, and bats. If you are attacked by these animals, it could prove dire to your survivability.

Be careful after constructing your heat reflector when building your fire. You will want to build your fire very slowly and not make it too big. Make sure you are outside the opening of the cave when you build the fire, and use caution while checking the entrance for large cracks. If you build a fire too big too quickly, it will cause the rocks overhead to crack and crumble.

Abandoned Buildings

Already constructed buildings can provide good shelter and excellent cover. Much like with caves, you should ensure that the structure is solid and intact and that there are no occupants. Set up an over watch position so that you are able to look for any signs of life. Apparently abandoned buildings are potentially dangerous to clear. If you are clearing a house or building by yourself, you risk being ambushed while negotiating multiple rooms connected to hallways that lead to more rooms. These corridors are especially dangerous as you risk being trapped in crossfire while trying to clear a passageway. Not every house is the same, and there may be unexpected obstacles blocking entryways. If noise is not an issue, a twelve-gauge shotgun or crowbar is usually enough to open any locked doors. If all else fails, kicking in a door and smashing a window will afford you entry into the building. Once inside the structure, take your time to determine whether or not you want to advance by taking the tactical pause to stop and look, listen, and smell for any signs of life. If you enter an empty dwelling that appears to be in good operable condition, and if there are stocked-up supplies such as plants, water, and animals, that is a good sign that there is a caretaker responsible for the establishment. Also look for other indicators such as recently used stoves still warm to the touch or running water and electrical devices. These are good gauges of nearby forces. If you find these signs, then utilizing extreme caution is highly recommended. In addition, look for other signs of either friendly or enemy occupants. After determining friend or foe, you may want to go back to your observation point to look for any signs of life to determine which times are best for raiding the house for supplies without any resistance. Keep in mind that if the resident has like-minded views and common beliefs, you may be able to gain a possible ally to your cause. If anything, the resident may have helpful information that could guide you toward your goals. Remember, when linking up with people you don't know in certain situations, you face the risk of opening up yourself to attack: stranger = danger.

After your shelter has served its purpose, you may or may not want to ensure that you don't leave any traces of your previous existence at the site. While avoiding anyone trying to hunt you and hurt you, pick up all your trash and remaining materials. If you brought it there, take it with you when you leave. Scatter the natural materials used to construct your shelter, such as branches and random vegetation. Cover up any holes that you have previously dug, and replace the topsoil that you previously used.

If you wish to leave clues behind for any people who may be looking for you in order to help you, leaving a message with the estimated distance of and directions to your next location would help immensely. Leave messages by shaving bark off a nearby tree and carving your message deep enough that it may not be easily wiped away. Never leave messages in the dirt, as it may be washed away by rain or blown away by strong winds. Leaving a message by using heavy objects such as rocks is a better method but still runs a chance of being disturbed. While en route to your next shelter site, leave markings by disturbing ground cover, snapping branches, and tying objects in an easily detectable location at eye level.

7

FIRE

Fire has a tendency to bring people together, especially when the weather is cold. Think about the times when you went camping. Everyone gathers around the fire, whether it's to sing songs, tell stories, or just sit around to gaze at the flames as they dance in the dark. The firepit is always the nucleus of any campsite.

I remember during Christmastime my dad would often start a fire in the fireplace when we would have other families over to visit. Randomly, people were drawn to its warmth. The next thing you knew, there would be a gathering of people just standing or sitting around in the living room, having conversations and telling stories. Although inspirational to fellowship, fire should be treated with caution and a sense of maturity.

Fire makes a huge impact on morale when out in the bush trying to survive. Fire serves as a way to stay warm, keep dry, purify water, cook your food, and help improve hunting tools. It also provides light in the looming darkness as the sun makes its final descent for the day. While standing up to a survival situation, the presence of a fire has a mysterious way of drowning out any perplexing thoughts of self-doubt. One of humankind's oldest and greatest achievements is the discovery of fire and the ability to wield its flame.

> **For no other foundation can anyone lay than that which is laid, which is Jesus Christ. Now if anyone builds on this foundation with gold, silver, precious stones, wood, hay, straw, each one's work will become clear; for the Day will declare it, because it will be revealed by fire; and the fire will test each one's work, of what sort it is. If anyone's work which he has built on it endures, he will receive his reward. If anyone's work is burned, he will suffer loss; but he himself will be saved, yet so as through fire.**
>
> **(1 Corinthians 3:11-15)**

There is nothing more important in this life than your faith in Jesus Christ. Jesus is your way into heaven (John 14:6), so when you accept Christ as your Lord and Savior, the greatest foundation that could ever be constructed is set. What you choose to build atop this foundation is on you. Because on that day when God on his throne judges all of humankind, your work will be put to the test with fire. We should all pray that our work will be pleasing to God and endure the test of fire. However, because of the perfect foundation of

Christ, even if your work in this life is burned and you experience loss, you are still a child of God to whom He has promised a reward.

> "And to give you who are troubled rest with us when the Lord Jesus is revealed from heaven with His mighty angels, in flaming fire taking vengeance on those who do not know God, and on those who do not obey the gospel of our Lord Jesus Christ" (2 Thessalonians 1:7-8).

At the end of the tribulation when Jesus returns with His angels, the death of all His saints will be avenged with fire. Remember, vengeance is for the Lord (Romans 12:19). Only people who do not have a personal relationship with Christ will be so cruel as to persecute Christians. People who are scornful and intent on doing evil will be consumed and cut off (Isaiah 20:29). Many people often think of Jesus returning and appearing the same way He did during His ministry on earth before being crucified and then resurrected. What people fail to realize is that His return will be glorious and truly awesome!

> "His head and hair were white like wool, as white as snow, and His eyes like a flame of fire" (Revelation 1:14).

When Jesus returns on His white horse with all His angels, His eyes will be like the flame of fire as He will have His sights set on the wicked and the unrepentant.

> **And a fire came out from the Lord and consumed the two hundred and fifty men**

who were offering incense. (Numbers 16:35)

So Elijah answered and said to the captain of fifty, "If I am a man of God, then let fire come down from heaven and consume you and your fifty men." And fire came down from heaven and consumed him and his fifty. Then he sent him another captain of fifty with his fifty men.

And he answered and said to him: "Man of God, thus has the king said, 'Come down quickly!'"

So Elijah answered and said to them, "If I am a man of God, let fire come down from heaven and consume you and your fifty men." And the fire of God came down from heaven and consumed him and his fifty.

Again, he sent a third captain of fifty with his fifty men. And the third captain of fifty went up, and came and fell on his knees before Elijah, and pleaded with him, and said to him: "Man of God, please let my life and the life of these fifty servants of yours be precious in your sight. Look, fire has come down from heaven and burned up the first two captains of fifties with their fifties. But let my life now be precious in your sight." (2 Kings 1:10-14)

Not only during the end times but right now we should all submit to God and avoid being rebellious. When we rebel against God, we risk being consumed in fire. God uses his prophet Elijah to demonstrate His awesome power. God can show Himself as fierce fire from heaven to grab people's attention. Some believe that in the case described in 2 Kings 1:10-14, the fire that consumed the captains and their fifty was lightning. Those who do not submit to God and worship Him risk being completely and utterly consumed by His fire.

> "And the Angel of the Lord appeared to him in a flame of fire from the midst of a bush. So he looked, and behold, the bush was burning with fire, but the bush was not consumed" (Exodus 3:2).

Other times when God decides to show himself to His obedient children, the angel of the Lord may appear as a fire that does not consume. When God appeared to Moses for the first time, he caught Moses's attention with fire, by not burning up the bush in the area that God had made holy. Moses couldn't help but be intrigued by the burning bush because of the simple fact that it was not being consumed by the fire. God successfully captured Moses's attention so that he could receive God's Word.

"But Peter followed Him at a distance, right into the courtyard of the high priest. And he sat with the servants and warmed himself by the fire" (Mark 14:54).

Peter was Jesus's proudest and most loyal disciple. When Jesus told Peter he would deny Him three times before the rooster crowed twice,

Peter refused to believe Jesus's prediction. Peter even went as far as to say that he would die before denying Jesus (Mark 14:27-31).

Peter was lacking in courage as he sat next to the fire, even after all the miracles he'd witnessed Jesus perform. He kept his distance from Jesus as He was arrested and taken to trial. While Peter was warming himself, he was listening in on the accusations being made against Jesus. After he was confronted three times by people who said he knew Jesus and was with Him as a disciple, the rooster crowed a second time, and Peter wept when he remembered what Jesus had said earlier (Mark 14:66-72).

It's easy to be proud and courageous when things are going our way in the absence of any real problems. Even amid the little things that cause distractions in our everyday lives, people tend to fall apart. The next time you are sitting by a fire to stay warm, take a moment to remember what Jesus told Peter before He was arrested. Instead of relying on our own strength in the flesh, we should pray for spiritual strength from the Holy Spirit so that when things get tough, we won't keep our distance from Jesus and the fire of the Holy Spirit will burn fiercely inside us.

When using fire in order to survive, you will need to consider whether or not it is worth it if other people happen to see its glow from a great distance. The best way to signal a rescue search party is to create a large fire that has the capability of providing a great amount of smoke. If you are in a situation where you are being pursued by people who wish to do harm to you, the smoke that your fire gives off can linger, and its scent can serve as a target indicator for anyone nearby. In addition, any left-behind remains of the fuel you used to feed the fire, such as wood, can give anyone honing in on your trail a fresh new starting point to begin looking for more clues as to where your most likely route may be.

No matter what kind of terrain and climate you are trying to survive in, you will eventually need the use of fire, even if you are being followed by an antagonist. Ultimately the use of fire can either save your life or become your definitive undoing. Once you have reached that point, your first thought should be why you need the fire in the first place. You should then consider how much time you have to build the fire. If darkness is fast approaching, you may want to begin gathering whatever materials and equipment are at your disposal. If you are in hostile circumstances trying to survive, you will most definitely want to know where your enemy is and whether or not they are interested in moving in on you specifically.

The three essential components for fire are material, heat, and oxygen. Without all three of these elements, you will not be able to build a fire. Three material elements of fire are tinder, kindling, and fuel.

Tinder consists of small combustible substances that can instantaneously be ignited easily by a spark or strong heat source. Some examples of tinder are thin shavings from a stick, dried dead grass, crumbled leaves, bark shavings, sawdust, and cotton. Pretty much anything in the wild that comes from trees and other plants that can be dried out and shaved or made into finer material can be used as tinder. It is important that all the materials used for your tinder touch each other but are not so compact that oxygen is not allowed to move freely between the materials.

If in the wilderness you are unable to locate something small enough and dry enough to use, any extra fabric that can be spared would be appropriate. Cutting a piece off the bottom of a shirt made of cotton or wool is permissible. Also check your pockets for any lint that may have been left over from your dryer at home after washing your clothes. While on the move, don't wait until you need tinder before you start looking for it. Your best ally in the woods is the ability to multitask so you can move toward your goals faster. You should always be thinking a few steps ahead of where your situation may lead you.

Kindling is the second element that you add to the tinder after the latter has produced a flame. This element must be applied almost instantly after the tinder has ignited. If you wait too long, the tinder could burn out before catching your kindling, and then you will be required to start the process all over again.

Examples of kindling include twigs, small branches, and larger branches or logs that have been split into smaller strips the diameter of a pencil. Ensure that the kindling you are using is dry. If the kindling does not snap easily, it may not be dry enough to use. Just as you ensure that you have tinder ahead of time, you should prepare kindling beforehand by stripping or shaving the outer layer or bark and storing the remains in a protective container such as a backpack or jacket pocket to allow for drying.

Fuel is the larger main element that will keep your fire going with less nurture. Just like your kindling, your fuel should be dry. The best fuel to use in the wild are thick branches as big around as your arm and as long as the distance from your wrist to your elbow. Once the fire becomes robust, you will be able to upgrade to larger branch sections or even small logs should your situation permit. Ultimately you will want to generate hot coals from your fuel to maintain your fire's health as you will be required to feed the fire more fuel.

The second component, heat, is just as crucial as the tinder, kindling, and fuel. Applying a heat source is done more in conjunction with tinder than it with kindling and fuel. The most common and useful heat source is matches and lighters. Matches and lighters are very easy to use and require hardly any practice to master. If you suspect that you may soon find yourself in a wilderness setting, you should consider taking along either matches or a lighter, or both. Whatever you decide, waterproofing your selected fire starter is always a very sound decision.

Other heat sources may be flint and steel, sparks, friction, and concentrated sunlight. These other methods are not as common as striking a match and should be explored and practiced frequently before they become a necessity. Just as you will not always have matches and lighters on your person, you will not always have a commercial flint and steel on hand to create a spark. It is a necessity to have previous experience and knowledge of which types of rocks and metals work in different situations. One of the hardest ways to create a heat source is by using friction. When in the wild, you will not always have perfectly dry branches to start a fire. One of the most often thought-of ways to create friction is to rub two sticks together. This method is very time-consuming and is extremely hard to master. After devoting a lot of time to rubbing two sticks together to create heat friction, you may become exhausted, frustrated, and demotivated. Having the patience to take a little more time to engineer a more efficient way of creating friction is imperative when fatigue and inadequate time are factors.

    A well-constructed method of starting a fire is a bow drill. There are six basic parts of a bow drill: (1) the bow, made from a small branches the length of your arm with string or rope tied at each end; (2) the drill, made from a stick or branch carved into a simple stake; (3) the bearing block, made from a simple block of wood with a depression cut into the center to allow pressure to be applied to the top of the drill; (4) the hearth board, made from a strip of wood with a depression and a V-shaped notch cut out of the depression (the hearth board is where the friction and tinder will meet with the bottom of the drill); (5) the baseboard, made from a strip of wood placed under the hearth board and used to contain the tinder and the embers generated by the friction; and (6) the tinder, which will supply the first stage of fuel required to build the fire. Essentially a bow drill is nothing more than a simple device powered by a small bow to drive a wooden stake back and forth in a drilling-like manner to create friction. The first five parts of a bow drill are what you will need to catch the tinder with a spark from the heat friction. Obviously you will want the other two elements of your fire on standby for when the tinder begins to smoke. Once you are set up and ready to begin, place your foot on top of the hearth board so to clamp them down, holding the hearth board and baseboard in place. You may now begin working the bow in a steady, sawing-like motion. Continue creating friction until you spot a sign of smoke.

Once you spot smoke, you will want to add the final desired component necessary for a flame, oxygen. While you are generating friction for your tinder, there is already an ample supply of oxygen to get things started. However, the appearance of smoke is an indication that oxygen is being used to create the burning reaction to the friction, in which case additional oxygen is required to maintain the momentum of this reaction. The best method for the survivor is to lightly blow into the tinder. If you blow too hard, you will most likely break up the tinder and push it out of position with your breath. Humans, of course, breathe in oxygen and exhale carbon dioxide. What you, the survivor, are doing is aiding the preexisting oxygen surrounding the area in catching fire to the tinder, allowing a constant flow until there is enough to create a flame. It is at this crucial moment that you will want to add kindling to the flame and thereby increase the amount of fuel. Keep in mind that the more fuel you add, the greater the oxygen supply to the fire you will need. Finally, as the fire progresses to its final stages, you will be able to add the prime size of fuel and maintain the fire's oxygen supply for a good while. In the event that the flame dies down and more firewood is needed, you may need to help get things started back up again with an oxygen resupply.

Suppose you already have your shelter constructed, such as a lean-to. In this case, you most likely have your overhead cover, a pine needle bed, and a decent heat shield fabricated ready to maintain your body heat through the night. If you are without a poncho, then your lean-to is most likely constructed from the branches you were able to scrounge. Now you are ready to build your fire. Before you start rubbing two sticks together in a caveman-like fashion, step back and take a moment to observe and assess your surroundings. You literally have built yourself a man-sized fire structure that you plan to sleep in with the intent of building a fire in the middle of it. It is important to take the necessary precautions when preparing the site in which you plan to make a fire.

The correct thing to do is to clear any existing brush that you do not need from the area. Loose leaves and pine needles have a really good chance of catching fire and being caught up in a moving breeze, carrying them upward to the ceiling of your shelter and setting the whole thing ablaze. Even if your overhead protection is just one poncho tied to some trees, you still run the risk that drifting burning leaves will melt your poncho. It may not catch the whole poncho on fire; however, it will burn a hole in your rain poncho, thus allowing water to leak through.

After clearing away the brush, scrape the surface soil away from the area where you plan to build your fire. The best method is to create a circular area of approximately three feet in diameter. If large stones are available, use them to surround the circular area to help contain the fire and prevent it from spreading. If no rocks are around, another good technique is to dig a trench around the circumference to separate the contained area from the floor of your shelter.

Aboveground fires are easy to create and are manageable to maintain. Apart from clearing out any combustible brush and topsoil, there is hardly any work involved for preparations. It is important that you position the wood you intend to use for your fires in an arrangement that provides optimal efficiency in radiating heat. The two most common and efficient methods are the teepee method and the log cabin method. Both methods operate the same way as their structures both revolve around the tinder and kindling and are primarily constructed with the initial series of fuel previous to starting the fire. The tepee is constructed in a circular manner at the base, where the logs are stacked upward at an angle and coming to a point. The log cabin is constructed with a rectangular base in which the logs are stacked horizontally on top of one another, thus creating a boxlike structure. These types of structures are extremely practical in a survival scenario as they both allow you to use wet wood once a fire has been created. The inner fire will have dried out the outer layer of wood by the time the inner layers of wood have expired.

Using 550 Cord

If time is not on your side and you need to build a fire in a pinch using friction, a good and simple method is the fire thong method. Use a dry strip of wood split down the middle. The split should be wedged open with another piece of wood. Lean the split branch or log at an angle on top of a rock, another log, or whatever is available. Run a strand of 550 cord through the split. Place tinder in the split, and vigorously pull the 550 cord back and forth in the same sawlike manner as with the bow drill technique. I recommend placing a baseboard with more tinder underneath and high enough to make contact with the upper tinder. When the lower tinder is ready, you will find it easier to place kindling on the bottom.

Making a Fire-Plow

Another simple technique for providing heat strong enough to produce flame is the fire-plow. This method is very easy to use. One of the best things about a fire-plow is that it produces its own tinder. All this technique requires is a flat wooden surface, such as a split log, and a shaft carved out of a stick. Create a trench down the middle of the flat surface, and use the shaft to plow back and forth until the sawdust particles become hot enough to ignite. As always, ensure that you have your kindling and fuel close by and readily available.

Using Binocular Lenses

If you have ever used a magnifying glass to incinerate ants, then you are already an expert in the use of your binocular lenses. With the availability of a powered lens, you have the potential to harness and concentrate the sun's rays to ignite your tinder. Other objects that can be used are camera lenses, telescope lenses, and the plastic bulb protector of a flashlight. You can also use the light bulb itself, given the proper angle. Whenever you allow the sun's rays to pass through such an object, light will be projected from the rays being condensed as it passes through. Varying the distance between the lens and the tinder will change the size of the light's radius. You want this light to be at its smallest as this will allow the rays to be focused on one spot. It won't take long before your tinder is ignited. This technique does not require a lot of skill. Most people master starting fires with a lens before they graduate from second grade.

    Just because you had an easy time starting your fire before nightfall while it was dry doesn't mean that you won't have to deal with rainy weather with strong gusts of wind later. You also don't want to be moving around in the dark, trying to gather up new supplies and starting all over.

    Before you actually start your fire, make sure that you have enough wood to last you through the night.

    Have a plan B in case you need to douse the fire.

8

SIGNAL

We live in an age where communications are seemingly instantaneous across nearly the entire planet. Because we live in the information age, people appear unable to function, let alone survive, without social media on their devices. We have the ability to keep track of our entire network of people with just the press of a button or the swipe of a finger across a screen. We are living in a time when infinite amounts of superficial information are within the reach of the majority of the earth's population. Daniel 12:4 reads, "But you, Daniel, shut up the words, and seal the book until the time of the end; many shall run to and fro, and knowledge shall increase."

This easily obtainable worldwide information is both good and bad. The good is that if someone is about to go into a situation that may involve survival, should something not work as planned, then their entire network of people are able to see what their plans were and their possible whereabouts by reading their latest posts. The bad is that we are living in a cement jungle full of dangerous people who suffer from a horrible addiction to texting while driving. Additionally, much of what is being taken in through the avenues of social media can become a huge distraction from the Word of God.

In most cases, help is almost always available throughout our communities in the United States. With the support of cellular telephones, any task can be summoned and completed with friends, family, and professional assistance. In the event of a flat tire, all you need to do is call your local roadside assistance company, and they will send you the help you need if you do not have a spare tire.

As you know, things don't always work out. Batteries die, and you always have the potential to find yourself alone and in need of assistance. In a survival situation, you may have to fabricate your own means of communicating with other people to secure your survival. Of course you always have the option of communicating with God—and God always answers prayers.

> **And it shall come to pass in the last days, says God,**
>
> **That I will pour out of My Spirit on all flesh;**
>
> **Your sons and your daughters shall prophesy,**
>
> **Your young men shall see visions,**
>
> **Your old men shall dream dreams.**

> **And on My menservants and on My maidservants**
>
> **I will pour out My Spirit in those days;**
>
> **And they shall prophesy.**
>
> —Acts 2:17–18

We are in the last days leading up to the end of days, the tribulation. As time goes on, we are increasingly heading toward a spiritual revival like no other throughout the United States and all over the world. The Bible says that every time someone accepts Christ and repents, there is joy in the presence of the angels of God (Luke 15:10). Imagine being on the roller coaster of Christianity at a theme park. Right now we are on the incline. Once we reach the top, things in our lives will accelerate to supernatural speeds.

When you are asleep, you are open to receiving a revelation from the Holy Spirit when you dream. That is why it is so important to pray before you go to bed. And when you first wake up, prayer, along with confirmation of scripture, is important so that you can make sure you understand what God is telling you. When Christians are obedient and read scripture in the Bible, they allow themselves to receive revelation from God's Word.

In these latter days, God is pouring out His Spirit on *all* flesh so that His children can receive His Word to do His will. Imagine that you have a new, unopened gallon of milk and you have to pour the milk in a hole the size of a golf ball without spilling it. You have no idea how deep the hole is, but there is a bottom. What you do know is that as you empty the jug, you get closer and closer to something you've been waiting for.

When you open a brand-new gallon of milk, at first you only tip it slightly so you don't make a mess. Then as the hole starts to fill up, you have to tip the jug more and more so the milk pours faster and faster. Eventually you end up holding the jug of milk completely upside down. Now imagine that this milk jug is full of the Holy Spirit and that it never runs out. Eventually the hole fills up and overflows with the Holy Spirit.

Right now, God is filling us with His Spirit. Eventually the hole fills up and overflows out of His people. However, some people choose to put on a lid to cover up their opening and refuse the Holy Spirit, much like in Exodus 8:15 when the pharaoh hardened his own heart. Then seals are opened, trumpets are sounded, and bowls will be poured. The battle of Armageddon is on the horizon.

During the tribulation, this spiritual revival will not cease, but there will be a falling away from faith in the church. And God will take away his restraints (2 Thessalonians 2:3-8; 1 Timothy 4:1). Right now, many people who freely worship Christ and claim to believe in Him have not had to endure persecution like others around the world currently endure today. During tribulation and persecution, all the people who claim Christ as their Lord and Savior will be tested like never before. Only those who have been filled with the Holy Spirit will truly believe in Christ as their Lord. Only true believers in Christ will resist the mark of the beast.

Now imagine that instead of a milk jug, there are seven angels in heaven with seven bowls.

Imagine that it's the very end of the seventh year of tribulation and the seventh trumpet is about to sound. The seven angels are waiting for the trumpet so they can pour their seven bowls of God's wrath, one after the other. Now the roller coaster is on the decline as it rapidly gains speed. There is no stopping it, just like there is nothing that Satan can do to stop God's judgment. When the roller-coaster ride reaches the bottom and is moving at its maximum speed, will you be called up to be with our Lord? If this is a question that you are unable to answer, you may be deficient in prophetic understanding given a lack of scripture in your life.

> **And so we have the prophetic word confirmed, which you do well to heed as a light that shines in a dark place, until the day dawns and the morning star rises in your hearts; knowing this first, that no prophecy of Scripture is of any private interpretation, for prophecy never came by the will of man, but holy men of God spoke as they were moved by the Holy Spirit. (2 Peter 1:19-21)**

> **Beware of false prophets, who come to you in sheep's clothing, but inwardly they are ravenous wolves. You will know them by their fruits. Do men gather grapes from thornbushes or figs from thistles? (Matthew 7:15-16)**

Driving around a dark country road in the middle of the night without headlights is dangerous and suicidal. So why would anyone want to go through this world without the prophecy of scripture that is in the Bible? The Bible in its entirety is the perfect Word of God. The words that are written in the Bible were written by holy people whom God chose to fill with the Holy Spirit as a guide to allow them to convey exactly what God's will on earth is.

Anything that you receive that is not in accordance with scripture is not from God but is from an agent of evil disguised in sheep's clothing. Even today, there are churches that claim to be of Christ but present false doctrine. Although there are no existing prophets alive today who are inspired to add to the complete Word of God, we know that the Holy Spirit inspires people to seek truth from the Word of God. God's Word is infallible.

> "So then faith comes by hearing, and hearing by the Word of God" (Romans 10:17).

The greatest responsibility that Christians are charged with is spreading the gospel of Jesus Christ. When you provide others with food, water, shelter, and warmth, they become more willing to receive what you have to say. If believers in Christ don't share the Word of God so that people can accept Christ, then food, water, shelter, and warmth are only mere speed bumps along the way to the inevitable: eternal death. We must know the Word of God and speak clearly and comprehensively when we share the gospel to ensure that the message is well received.

> "But as many as received Him, to them He gave the right to become children of God, to those who believe in His name: who were born, not of blood, nor of the will of flesh, nor of the will of man, but of God" (John 1:12).

As believers in Christ, we should want to increase the size of our family, that is, our spiritual family. No matter who it is or what they've done, whenever someone accepts Christ as their personal Lord and Savior, they become a child of God. When we become Christians and put down our own will to carry out the will of God, we all become brothers and sisters in Christ.

> "Again I say to you that if two of you agree on earth concerning anything that they ask, it will be done for them by My Father in heaven. For where two or three are gathered together in My name, I am there in the midst of them" (Matthew 18:19-20).

During the last days, whom you surround yourself and network with could mean the difference between life and death. It will be paramount that Christians find ways to link up with one another to commune. It takes just a few Christians in agreement to ask God for something and it will be done because Jesus will be right there with them.

Just like in some communist countries around the world today, Christians in the United States more than likely will be forced to worship and praise in "the underground church" during the tribulation. However, according to 2 Timothy 1:7,

"You are the light of the world. A city that is set on a hill cannot be hidden." I believe that like in many countries under martial law, curfews will be emplaced and military-age males will, at the least, not be allowed to gather in large groups. At these times it will be most necessary to spread the light of Christ. It is important to start building a Christian network with your brothers and sisters now because you never know when you yourself may have to signal fellow believers for help.

One of the most effective ways to signal for help in a survival situation is by using fire. The previous covers the different techniques and skills for creating a fire in the wilderness. The best way to accomplish this is by building a "log cabin" type structure out of logs considerably bigger than those you would use for your survival campfire. Use a fair amount of tinder and kindling in the middle of the log cabin structure. Cover the entire structure with lots of green leaves and pine needles to create smoke. Leave a hole at the top of the structure to provide easy access for adding more tinder and kindling. You may have to continually reinforce the structure with the logs that you will eventually use to fuel the fire.

Remember, always have a quick fire-starting method on standby in the event that friendly search parties are suspected to be nearby; do not waste an opportunity for a successful rescue. At night you have a greater chance of being seen and rescued if you have a large fire. During the day your best option is to throw the fresh green pine needles and grass on top of the fire as this will create smoke for others to see from a great distance. Keep in mind, though, that both day and night techniques have the potential to attract unwanted attention if you are in a possible hostile area or situation.

Another good technique is to use what the military calls a VS-17 Panel for near recognition. These are large squares of canvas cut into a square. The canvas is olive drab or green on one side and blaze orange on the other side. The blaze or hunter orange will do a good job of standing out in your surroundings while you are in the wilderness. Some things I like to pack with me when I go out in the woods is a bright orange bandanna and a baseball cap with blaze-orange material sewn on the inside.

In the event that you are not successful in building a fire and you have no blaze-orange materials, signal mirrors are a good way to reflect light up toward the sky when airplanes fly overhead. Hold the mirror in one hand, positioning it to face the sun and the approaching aircraft. Hold your opposite hand in a position to form a *V* shape between your thumb and index finger. Angle the mirror so light is shown reflecting into the *V* of your hand. You will use the *V* of your hand as an aiming point or sight picture while adjusting the reflected glare of the index point of the *V* shape toward your target (the airplane). The index point is when the aircraft can be seen in the *V* while the reflected light is shining through the opening of the *V* and all three are in alignment. If you have the foresight to pack a signal mirror, which most store-bought emergency kits include, have one available in all your vehicles, purses, day packs, etc.

If you do not have a proper signal mirror on hand, try to find something that you can use instead. Even if your cell phone has no battery power, the screen can still be used to reflect light. Other common items that may be on hand are watches, eyeglasses, and jewelry. If you are on foot and trying to find shelter or seeking civilization, look for anything that could be used along the way, such as pieces of glass or scrap metal.

If you are on foot and on the move, and you know other people from your group are actively looking for you or are known to be in the same area and you are looking for them, use trail signs. This is a tactical method as trail signs are concealed at ground level but visible from the air. When using available materials such as logs, scrapped pieces of metal, or poles, use size and ratio shapes to create signs. Size and ratio shapes should be big enough for the pilot of an aircraft to spot at a far distance and should be laid out to match the same shape of letters as they would be written on paper. Trail signs are based on simple symbols, as follows:

- ▶ V = Requires assistance
- ▶ X = Requires medical assistance
- ▶ N = No or negative
- ▶ Y = Yes or affirmative
- ▶ → = Proceed in this direction

The use of audio signals such as voice or yelling, a whistle, and weapon fire is also very effective for signaling someone nearby. This is not a tactical method, but it can produce immediate results. Use what you can to make a whistle. The top of an acorn shell or a bottle cap can aid you in this. Take the hollowed object and make a V shape with the use of your thumbs. All edges of the item should be sealed except the V made by your thumbs. Blow into and slightly across the V-shaped opening to create a high-pitched whistle sound. This is something you may want to practice before it becomes necessary.

Another great way to provide for your family or community is to become a licensed ham amateur radio operator. Not only is a ham radio a great tool for maintaining communications during a complete and chaotic shutdown of society, but also it will allow you to help emergency personnel to find and help people in the event of a natural disaster if for some reason the phone towers go down. Other communications devices that will serve you well are two-way radios / walkie-talkies, your current cellular telephone, Tracfones, and even satellite phones.

Your cell phone should be your number one method for emergency comms. It already has all your contact information, and your contacts should already have your information. It is also a good idea to write that information down on paper and keep it in a safe place. Your cell phone and other electronics are, however, at risk if there is any kind of natural or man-made EMP (electromagnetic pulse), so it's good to always have a backup device.

An EMP is a surge of electromagnetic waves that can short out any electronic device with a circuit board, which is just about anything that runs on batteries or electricity nowadays. Even cars made after 1987 are at risk and will not be able to operate in the event of an EMP. New cars have computer circuit boards even if they don't have all the latest features. The causes of EMPs may be either natural or man-made. Large solar flares from the sun can send a large enough electromagnetic pulse to affect earth from outer space. A nuclear explosion can also be used as an EMP. In fact, the explosion doesn't even have to hit the ground to be effective.

There are ways to protect your electronic devices by storing them in Faraday cages or bags, which employ a copper lining meant to divert the EMP, similar to a storm cage diverting the electrical current of a lightning strike. An electromagnetic pulse and lightning are very similar in nature. Faraday bags can be commercially purchased however, but they can also be fabricated. One of the most popular methods is to use a metal trash can. As long as you have a nonconductive interior lining such as cardboard or rubber matting, the current should bypass any technological device stored inside the bag. Other quick supplies you may have on have on hand are military-grade ammo cans. Old microwave ovens are believed to be a good protective barrier from an EMP as well.

If things really take a turn for the worse, then you may have to rely on other, unconventional techniques. There is a plethora of situations you may run into that may require you to think outside the box. Things to consider and perhaps practice ahead of time with your family, friends, church members, et al., are different communications techniques that may be a little outdated and not as common as they used to be, such as the following:

- Learning Morse code
- Learning how to operate a ham radio
- Learning the phonetic alphabet
- Learning how to read military time
- Learning hand and arm signals

9

FIRST AID

Everyone should know first aid. All rangers are required to know more than the basic first-responder techniques. However, mastering the basics will put you way above the power curve, and basic first aid is something that you can practice at home on your own. I recommend getting together with your local fire department or another expert you trust to see if classes are available to receive formal basic education from an instructor such as an EMT.

Get others involved as well. Do not rely on just one person to know all the medical information. That one person could be the next person who needs to receive treatment. Always strive to learn more so as to better yourself with lifesaving first aid.

I once had to conduct medical training by running through a stress lane while carrying a patient and then going into a shut garage in the pitch-black. Before my eyes could even adjust to the dark, I was handed an IV kit and told I had to initiate an IV and saline lock, which entails finding a vein and inserting a needle.

All the while, there were role-players yelling, acting hurt, crying for help, and being unruly. There were even other soldiers outside the garage, banging on the walls and attempting to overwhelm me. Thankfully, because I'd had lots of training and mental conditioning, their attempts to distract me were of no avail and I was able to accomplish my task.

Of all aspects or phases of survival, first aid takes priority in the event than you or a member of your group is injured. First aid is the first care given to an injured person before someone with professional medical training is available to continue medical care. In the last days, we will be the first responders of Christ. God is the ultimate care provider.

> "And that very hour He cured many of infirmities, afflictions, and evil spirits; and to many blind He gave sight" (Luke 7:21).

Besides feeding people, one of the great miracles that Jesus performed to increase faith and demonstrate the love of God was healing the sick. Only perfect, true, unconditional love has this much power to glorify God.

> **When he saw Jesus from afar, he ran and worshiped Him. And he cried out with a loud voice and said, "What have I to do with You, Jesus, Son of the Most High God? I implore you by God that you do not torment me."**

> **For He said to him, "Come out of the man, unclean spirit!" Then He asked him, "What is your name?"**
>
> **And he answered, saying, "My name is Legion; for we are many." Also he begged Him earnestly that He would not send them out of the country. (Mark 5:6–10)**

Even the evil spirits recognize the healing power of Jesus. As soon as Jesus showed up, the man worshipped Him. The evil demonic spirits even pleaded with Jesus not to torment them. The power of the Most High God is so great that it is able to cast out legions of demonic spirits.

> "And when He had called His twelve disciples to Him, He gave them power over unclean spirits, to cast them out, and to heal all kinds of sickness and all kinds of disease" (Matthew 10:1).

When we become Christians, we are literally followers of Christ, which makes us one of His disciples. As children of God, we are filled with the Holy Spirit through our faith. The Holy Spirit is the power of God. Because of our faith and acceptance in Christ, we have power over unclean spirits, sickness, and disease. When we put hands on our loved ones and pray over them (Acts 8:17), we are allowing the Holy Spirit to work though us. When we speak against unclean spirits and disease, we are using the Holy Spirit to cast these spirits out. We are not the ones who are doing these things; rather, it is the power of the Holy Spirit that comes from our acceptance of Christ. Even though you may not see immediate results, you should know that God's miracles are already at work and that God's plan is perfect for everything in your life.

> "Heal the sick, cleanse the lepers, and raise the dead, cast out demons. Freely you have received, freely give" (Matthew 10:8).

Jesus commands us to go out and heal the sick and cure them of disease. He even commands us to raise the dead and cast out demons. This is not an option; it is the will of God. Otherwise Jesus would have not commanded this of us. As followers of Christ, we should feel compelled to pray over people in need of both physical and spiritual healing. In addition, salvation cannot be purchased, and neither can the Holy Spirit that heals. The Holy Spirit has already been freely given through the perfect gift of Jesus Christ's death and resurrection (Acts 8:18–22). Jesus says, "It is easier for a camel to go through the eye of a needle than for a rich man to enter the kingdom of God" (Mark 10:25). Therefore, we shouldn't ask for payment or favor from those we heal in the name of Jesus.

> "When an unclean spirit goes out of a man, he goes through dry places, seeking rest; and finding none, he says, 'I will return to my house from which I came.' And when he comes, he finds it swept and put in order. Then he goes and takes with him seven other spirits more wicked than himself, and

they enter and dwell there; and the last state of that man is worse than the first" (Luke 11:24–26).

When addicts undergo treatment and rehabilitation, sometime later they are at risk of relapse, and when they relapse, their addiction is even greater than it was before. Whether it be addition to drugs, sex, alcohol, or even food, doctors, medicine, and therapy only serve as temporary treatment of the symptoms. Often, people who are under attack by the demonic spirit of addiction fall deeper and deeper into their unhealthy lifestyle, and unfortunately this sometimes results in their deaths.

When you see someone who is in desperate need of healing, maybe even other Christians, you need to heal them permanently in Jesus's name with the Holy Spirit that is within you. Once that person is healed, you now have a crucial situation on your hands.

The only way to ensure that unclean spirits do not return with greater numbers and move back in is to establish a new residence. The only new residence strong enough to occupy and keep out evil is the Holy Spirit. When people accept Christ, they have the Holy Spirit living within them. "Do you not know that you are the temple of God and that the Spirit of God dwells in you" (1 Corinthians 3:16)? It is in that decisive moment after healing takes place when Christians have the initiative and are to finish the job by helping usher the Holy Spirit into someone's life by preaching the gospel of Jesus Christ.

It is important to make sure that you follow specific lifesaving steps when practicing first aid. These steps are to clear the airway, stop the bleeding, and prevent. shock.

There are three types of bleeding. With arterial bleeding there is bright red blood that spurts out of the wound with each heartbeat. Venous bleeding flows steadily and is dark red. The last and least threatening is capillary bleeding, which only just oo0zes slowly out the wound. It is very important to make sure that a wound is treated immediately so it will not get infected and create even bigger problems.

Bleeding

In order to stop the bleeding, you will need to apply a field dressing or battle dressing. A battle dressing is a large bandage constructed of thin fabric with a large pad of absorbent cloth sewn in the middle of the strip. Field dressings can be used as pressure dressings. Before placement of the field dressing, however, compact gauze should be placed over the wound. Then apply manual firm pressure on the dressed wound for five to ten minutes. Elevate the limb above the heart. Apply the pressure dressing. Apply tourniquet. Apply a tourniquet by putting it around the limb between the injury and the heart, two to four inches above the wound. You do not ever want to put a tourniquet on any joint. It will not let you stop the bleeding. Apply the tourniquet as tight as it takes in order to stop the bleeding. Do not ever use a wire or a string. Do not loosen a tourniquet unless you are a medical professional. The loss of too much blood will put the patient into shock. Shock is the body's reaction to inadequate blood flow to the vital organs and tissues. If shock is not treated in a timely manner, it could very likely cause an injured person to die. Shock can cause death even if the initial injury was not life-threatening. One sign of shock is cool, pale, and damp, clammy skin. Also, the person in shock will have confusion, nausea, or vomiting. They will have restlessness or nervousness and obviously will have experienced loss of blood. Thirst, fast breathing, fainting spells, excessive perspiration, and blotched or bluish skin around the mouth and lips are also common signs of shock.

The best way to treat shock is by moving the injured person under some type of cover. Lay the casualty on their back and elevate their legs. You will need to loosen their clothing at the neck, waist, ankles, and feet. As you try to keep the casualty calm, monitor the person to make sure that you are not chilling them or overheating them.

Burns

Besides bleeding wounds, you may also encounter burn wounds. The four types of burn wounds are electrical, thermal, chemical, and laser. You must keep these wounds clean and dry and continue to place fresh dressings on them. There are three degrees of burns: first, second, and third. A first-degree burn is marked by reddening of the skin. With a second-degree burn, you will see blisters. A person with a third-degree burn will have charred skin.

Airway Obstruction

It is very important to make sure that the airway is not obstructed. In combat, the most common cause of airway blockage in an unconscious person is the person's own tongue, along with gum, food, or chewing tobacco. You may be required to place a nasopharyngeal tube to help clear the airway. A nasopharyngeal tube is a rubber tubular device that is used by placing it through one of the victim's nostrils to open up an airway as the tube passes into the throat behind the tongue.

CPR

If the victim has stopped breathing and has lost their heartbeat, you will be required to perform cardiopulmonary resuscitation or CPR. You perform CPR by breathing for the victim using mouth-to-mouth, an action referred to as breaths.

You also make a fist and place the opposite hand over your fist to assist in pushing just below the sternum. This action is referred to as pumps.

Directives regarding the ratio of breaths to pumps vary. One method is to apply fifteen pumps for every two breaths. Another method is to apply five pumps for every one breath. Either way, any CPR, even incorrect CPR, is better than no CPR. CPR should last as long as it needs to or until a doctor tells you to stop or you are relieved by another person. You should continue doing CPR at least until you cannot physically do it any longer or when, of course, the patient begins to breathe again on their own.

If the person is conscious and aware but cannot breathe, they may give the universal hand and arm signal for choking. They do this by placing the hands, one overlapping one the other, over their throat as if being choked. If they give this signal, they may require the Heimlich maneuver. Conduct the Heimlich maneuver by walking behind the patient. While standing behind the person, wrap both of your arms around their midsection.

Make a fist and then grab your fist with your other hand. While doing this, place both hands below the sternum but above the belly button and thrust your hands back and up against the patient's abdomen with sudden strong pressure.

For toddlers and babies, the Heimlich maneuver is conducted in a different manner, but the desired result is the same. Place the infant facedown on your forearm. Support the infant with your fingers on his or her neck and chin. Tilt your hand so that the infant's head is lower than his or her chest. With your other hand, use the palm to deliver five pats on the infant's back. If nothing is dislodged and falls out, then maneuver the infant onto his or her back on a flat surface such as the floor or a table. Use two fingers to deliver five chest thrusts below the nipple line and in line with the breastbone. Repeat the cycle of five pats and five chest thrusts until the airway is clear. If the infant becomes unconscious, immediately begin CPR. When I first learned child CPR for infants as a Boy Scout, the method was to reach inside the infant's mouth with a finger and try to scoop out the object. However, with research having been done over the years, it is now universal teaching that if you do that, you risk lodging the object even deeper, so this method is no longer practiced.

There are two types of injuries that can be induced from surviving in the wilderness based on temperature and climate. Heat injuries and cold injuries can occur all year long. It is important to know that even though heat injuries are more common in the summer, you can still become dehydrated and have heat exhaustion in the winter, as well as suffer from hypothermia in the summer months of the year.

Hot Weather Injuries

Heat injuries are brought on by the general dehydration of the body that is induced by loss of water and salt by overexertion of oneself in the heat. There are three types of heat injuries: heat cramps, heat exhaustion, and heatstroke.

Heat cramps are muscle cramps that are induced by lack of water intake. Indications of heat cramps are muscle cramps in the legs, arms, and abdomen. Heat cramps is the first sign that you are becoming a heat casualty. If you experience heat cramps, take a break from whatever you are doing to move into the shade, drink some cool water, and loosen some clothing to allow air to flow.

If you ignore the signs of heat cramps and continue to do work without any intake of water, you could easily become a casualty of heat exhaustion. The first sign of heat exhaustion is pale, moist, cool, clammy skin. This is followed by a headache along with muscle cramps, excessive sweating, weakness, nausea, and dizziness. You will have the urge to defecate with chills, rapid breathing, confusion, and tingling of the hands or feet. The treatment for heat exhaustion is much like the treatment for heat cramps, only now you should immediately drink at least two quarts of water and elevate your legs. If you fail to monitor someone with heat exhaustion, conditions could worsen.

Heatstroke is the most severe of all the heat-related conditions, and once you've had it, you run an even greater risk of getting it again.

A person with heatstroke will suffer similar conditions as the previous two heat injuries, only now the casualty will have dry skin and will stop being able to sweat. The injured person will feel hot with a rapid pulse rate. The same indications as heat exhaustion will be present, such as headache, dizziness, vomiting, mental confusion, and weakness, only now this injury will induce seizures. The best way to treat a person who is a heatstroke casualty is to immerse their entire body with the coldest water available on-site. Then you should remove the person's clothing and continue wetting their entire body while fanning them. Transport the injured person to the nearest medical facility.

Cold Weather Injuries

While surviving outdoors, spending long durations of spent in cold and wet environments without proper heat sources to keep warm and dry can be catastrophic for your health. As warm-blooded mammals, humans are naturally equipped to maintain body temperature and keep warm to a certain degree. However, if a person becomes wet, they stand a far greater chance of getting a cold weather injury, even in the warm months of the year. A basic reminder to use for preventing cold and wet weather injuries when surviving is the acronym COLD: keep it Clean, avoid Overheating, wear Loose clothing in multiple layers, and keep it Dry. Much like hot weather injuries, cold weather injuries are progressive and, when ignored during the early stages, can have a devastating effect and result in dire consequences as you freeze while trying to stay alive.

There are five types of cold and wet weather

injuries: frostbite, hypothermia, immersion foot or trench foot, chilblain, and snow blindness. Frostbite is the actual freezing of a part of your body. Signs of frostbite include loss of sensation or a numb feeling in any part of the affected area of the body; sudden whitening of the skin in the affected area followed by a momentary tingling feeling; redness of the skin in light-skinned people, and grayness of the skin in dark-skinned people; swollen and or tender areas; loss of previous feeling of pain in the affected area; pale, yellow, waxy-looking skin; and a frozen area that feels solid or wooden to the touch. The best way to treat frostbite is to warm the area at the first sign of frostbite with your hands under your arms or abdomen. For your face, ears, or nose, cover with your hands. For your hands, place them inside your clothing close to your body.

For your feet, place your bare feet against the body of another person. Keep extra gloves and socks against your body. Keep these dry, and switch them out often. Wool socks and wool gloves will help keep you warm even when wet. You will need to loosen tight clothing and take of any jewelry so it will not constrict any swollen areas. Cover up with a blanket or some type of dry material. Do *not* soak the frostbitten area, rub with snow, expose to extreme heat source, or rub or move the frostbitten area to increase circulation. Do *not* smoke tobacco or drink alcohol. Do *not* treat the area if you need to walk or travel to receive further treatment.

Hypothermia is the lowering of the body temperature faster than it can produce heat. There are two types of hypothermia: mild and severe. The casualty is cold. Shivering stops, but the body temperature is still low. Consciousness may be altered. Movement is uncoordinated. Shock and coma may set in as a result of lower body temperatures. The treatment for hypothermia is to immediately rewarm the body evenly with a heat source. Keep the person dry, and protect them from the elements. Warm liquids may be gradually given if the victim is conscious. Be prepared to start basic life support measures. Seek medical help immediately as the injured person must be treated as soon as possible. You can get hypothermia in the warm or hot months of the year, especially if you are wet during nighttime hours.

Immersion foot or what is more commonly known as trench foot occurs between 32 degrees and 50 degrees. The affected parts of the body are cold, numb, and free of pain. Then the parts become hot with burning and shooting pains. Advanced stages include pale skin with a bluish tint and decreased pulse. Blistering, swelling, heat, hemorrhages, and gangrene may follow. This injury is a result of long exposure of the feet to wet and cold. Inactive feet in damp or wet socks and boots or tightly laced boots that impair circulation can also cause immersion foot. The treatment is to rewarm the feet by gradually exposing them to hot air. Do not massage. Do not moisten. Do not apply heat or ice. Protect from future trauma. Keep dry and don't walk. Seek medical treatment.

Chilblain is a mild form of frostbite. Most people who have been outside in the snow have had this before. It is not uncommon. Affected areas are red, swollen, hot, tender, and itchy. More exposure leads to blisters or bleeding skin lesions. The proper treatment is to rewarm the area with body heat. Do not rub or massage the area.

Snow blindness is pain in or around the eyes after prolonged exposure in an ice field or snowfield. This can happen in cloudy weather as well. The symptoms are a sensation of grit or sand in the eyes that feels worse when the eyeball moves. Other signs include watering of the eyes, redness of the eyes, headache, and pain upon exposure to light. Seek medical aid. This injury is not permanent and will go away within two days. Prevent it by wearing sunglasses or constructing slits in front of your eyes by creating a mask with whatever material is available.

Fractures

The two most common types of fractures are open (compound) and closed (simple). An open fracture is a broken bone that breaks through the skin. The first thing that should be done for an open fracture is to stop the bleeding. Signs and symptoms of fractures are pain at the site, discoloration, and deformity. Immobilize fractures to prevent further damage from the sharp edges of the bone moving and cutting tissue, muscle, blood vessels, and nerves. Doing this reduces pain and helps prevent and control shock.

Splint the broken bone by taking two straight solid objects such as sticks or wooden boards and placing them on both sides of the limb. Take multiple strands of cloth, bandannas, etc. (two at a minimum), and wrap them around the boards and the limb, then tie them off. Do not wrap directly over the fractured area.

10

FIELD CRAFT

Field craft refers to the techniques and other implied supportive skills that contribute to maintaining and achieving your survival pattern. A large part of field craft requires the ability to travel while remaining undetected. Field craft allows you to observe what lies ahead before you are committed to enter into a situation you don't want to be in.

Snipers across the board rely heavily on their field craft skills to complete their missions and stay alive in the field. The field may involve either training or real-world scenarios conducted outdoors or "in the field." Either way, if a sniper is weak in this area, they have a great chance of being combat ineffective if they are identified before they even start their missions. Snipers and rangers alike spend much time in field training, honing their field craft before it becomes a required task for real-world success. The more you practice these skills, the more they will come to you automatically when you need them most.

Just like snipers in a non-permissive combat environment, Christians need to watch their step to avoid persecution. Of course, just like anything else that takes place in the survival pattern, it all begins and ends with prayer. The last thing you want to do in the event that you have to leave your home is to stick out like a sore thumb because you are wandering around, lost. If you appear to be an easy target, you will be treated as such.

> "Your ears shall hear a word behind you, saying, 'This is the way, walk in it,' whenever you turn to the right hand or whenever you turn to the left" (Isaiah 30:21).

As a Christian, the more you learn to trust in the Holy Spirit, which speaks revelation to you, the more you will be able to do what's right and walk in righteousness. Sometimes you will hear that little voice inside you that is your gut instinct to do good.

> "But the Helper, the Holy Spirit, whom the Father will send in My name, He will teach you all things, and bring to your remembrance all things that I said to you" (John 14:26).

You have the Holy Spirit within you because you believe in Jesus Christ. When you study the Word of God to establish a more meaningful relationship with Christ, it fuels the Holy Spirit. When you display this obedience, the Holy Spirit also reminds you of the things that Jesus taught when you need to be reminded most to have a sound mind.

> "However, when He, the Spirit of truth, has come, He will guide you into all truth; for He will not speak on His own authority, but whatever He hears He will speak; and He will tell you things to come" (John 16:13).

Any revelation that was sent from God to you, whether in a vision or in a dream, only speaks the truth and is only sent to guide and help you. It's up to you to listen to His Word and to trust in His will. Anything you see that is a lie or damaging is of the devil.

> "Give no regard to mediums and familiar spirits; do not seek after them, to be defiled by them: I am the Lord your God" (Leviticus 19:31).

During the end times, agents of evil will try to distract you and attempt to lead you astray into darkness. Beware of demonic entities. If it is not of God, then it is of evil. Only God can guide you to truth, which leads to eternal life (John 14:6).

Terrain Association

A map is a graphic representation of a portion of the earth's surface drawn to scale, as seen from above. Maps use colors, symbols, and labels to represent features, both natural and man-made, found on the ground. The colors used on a map are usually red, blue, green, black, and red-brown. Red is the color that assists the reader in identifying certain cultural features such as political areas, major roads, and boundaries. Blue is used to ID bodies of water such a streams, rivers, lakes, and swamps. Green IDs majorly vegetated areas, such as wooded areas and vineyards. Black is used to indicate man-made features like buildings and roads and is labeled in the legend of the map as such. Red-brown is used to help depict elevation. It is the color used to draw contour lines on a topographic map.

Contour lines are imaginary lines drawn on topographic maps that portray terrain features in a way that allows them to be measured in terms of elevation. The value of the contour line's contour interval is in the elevation guide, which is the vertical distance between the highest and lowest points of adjacent contour lines.

So, for example, if the value of the contour lines is thirty-five meters, then that is the distance interval between the lines that are drawn. With that being said, looking at it visually, the more spread out the space between the adjacent contour lines, the flatter the terrain is on the ground. The more condensed the lines are, the steeper the terrain will be.

Using contour lines and their intervals allows you to determine different terrain features. There are five major, three minor, and two supplementary terrain features. The five major terrain features are hills, saddles, valleys, ridges, and depressions.

- ▶ A hill is an area of high ground. A hill is shown on the map by contour lines forming

concentric circles. The inside of the smallest enclosed circle is the hilltop.
- A saddle is a dip or low point between two high areas or hills and mountains. A saddle is depicted in an hourglass shape between two hills when drawn by contour lines.
- A valley is a groove in the land, usually formed by a stream or river. Valleys have contour lines that look as if they are V-shaped and sometimes even appear to be U-shaped on the map.
- A ridge or ridgeline is a sloping line of high ground. Ridgelines look like a row of hilltops on a map.
- A depression is a sinkhole or a low point in the ground. Depressions have contour lines that are close together have tick marks facing inward toward low ground.

The three minor terrain features are draws, spurs, and cliffs:

- A draw is pretty much just a small valley. Draws have contour lines that are U- and V-shaped and that point to higher ground.
- A spur is a short ridge. Spurs are also U- and V-shaped, but they point to lower ground.
- A cliff is a vertical or near-vertical terrain feature that suddenly drops from a higher elevation to a lower elevation. Cliffs contour lines that are very close together and that sometimes touch.

The two supplementary terrain features are cuts and fills:

- ▶ A cut is a man-made feature that cuts through high ground and is often in a level bed used for constructing roads and railroad tracks.
- ▶ A fill is a man-made feature that fills in low areas and is often a level bed used for the construction of roads and railroad tracks.

So now that you know how to identify different objects and terrain features, the question is, how do you identify the location of these features on a map in relation to your location? With regular street maps, this is relatively easy to do because all you have to do is follow the roads and signs. However, if you foresee being in a position where you don't want to be noticed in the open or you are not presently anywhere near roads and street signs, you may want to invest in a grid map of your area.

Main grid lines that run from north to south and east to west are spaced apart in intervals of 1,000 meters. These lines that are parallel to the equator and the prime meridian create 1,000 meter × 1,000 meter areas on the map called grid squares. Based on the size of the map you are using, the grid squares are drawn to scale to accurately represent the locations you are trying to find on the map. At the bottom of the map, there is a diagram that displays the ratio of the distance covered on the map to the distance covered on the ground within a grid square. So, if the distance diagram states that this ratio is 1:50,000, then you know that every centimeter on the map equals 50,000 centimeters (or 500 meters) on the ground.

The lines used to create these grid squares are numbered using two-digit numbers. The numbers of one north-to-south-running grid line and one east-to-west-running grid line are used in combination with each other to describe one specific grid square labeled with a four-digit coordinate. So if you are looking at a square and wish to know its location, you first need to identify the left north-and-south-running line and the bottom east-and-west-running line. When doing this, remember to read them together in order from the right side and up. For example, if your left line is 17 and your bottom line is 92, then that grid square is: 1792, which will put you within 1,000 meters of that area. To narrow it down to a 100-meter area, you use a 6-digit coordinate, and to narrow it down even more to a 10-meter area, you could use an 8-digit coordinate. And to be even more precise, you should use a 10-digit coordinate, which will put you within 1 meter of what you are trying to locate on the map. Just by looking on the map if you were in a situation where you required rescuing, you could make a guess within 100 meters and more than likely put a search party or aircraft in relatively close proximity to your area.

    In order to figure out the more precise eight- and ten-digit coordinate, you need to use a protractor, which is a tool that helps you to measure out a more specific location within a grid square. The protractor is a square-shaped transparent plastic cutout that has index markings laid out and revolving around the center crosshair that divides a 360-degree circle into units of angular measurements. Apart from plotting precise points on a map, the 360-degree measurement is a useful tool to help you figure out a desired azimuth. An azimuth is a horizontal angle measured in a clockwise manner from a north baseline used to express the direction in which you would like to travel. In other words it gives a directional reading in degrees in relation to north, south, east, and west. Protractors can also be used as rulers to measure distances on the map.

Along with the azimuth, you need a compass to point you in the right direction as everything appears on the ground. A compass is a navigational device used to acquire an azimuth in either degrees or mills with the use of a magnetic north-seeking arrow. Now that you know where you are on the map and you have an azimuth, your compass tells you which direction your azimuth is in relation to that point, so you can begin walking in the right direction.

If you do not have a compass or a protractor, there are other ways you can determine cardinal direction. Sunrise (east) and sunset (west) is one such way. You may also use the stick and shadow method. Place a stick in the ground or a straight needle into a piece of paper to cast a shadow. At first lightly mark the tip of the shadow that the stick creates. Then at every thirty-minute interval until last light, mark the tip of the shadow and write down the time of each point. Connect all the dots to form an arch. The point of the arch closest to the stick or shadow device is the direction of north from that position. This is time-consuming, but it is more accurate than trying to keep track of the sun's movement while you are on the move. So, if you are stationary in a survival situation and you need to actively do something to keep yourself motivated, this is a great technique for doing that.

Using a wristwatch is another way to gain some

sort of sense of cardinal direction. If you are located in the Northern Hemisphere, point the hour hand at the sun. The direction of south is halfway between the hour hand and the twelve o'clock position. You may use this method with a digital watch by simply visualizing where the hour hand would be according to what time it is. While in the Southern Hemisphere, point the twelve o'clock position toward the sun. Halfway between the twelve o'clock position and hour hand is north. Again, you may use a digital watch if that's what is available to you.

Although in a survival situation traveling at night is not recommended, if the situation dictates travel, using the North Star is another basic way to find the direction of north. It is located just off to the right of where the Big Dipper opens up.

It is no easy feat stepping out into the unknown with few devices. Many say that the best thing to do is to stay put and signal for help. However, not every survival situation will allow you to remain static when there is looming danger. After reading this, you should have a fairly solid basic understanding of how land navigation works. People spend many years perfecting the art of land navigation and orienteering. Personally, I've been doing it ever since grade school when I was a Boy Scout. Now that you are able to identify the key terrain features on a map, you have the major piece of the puzzle in place. When you master using a protractor and compass along with terrain association, you will be able to accurately and confidently travel through wilderness areas without having to rely on roads and street signs.

Of course, as with anything else survival

related, don't let an actual life-or-death situation be the first time you ever do this. Take classes and find other ways to practice these skills ahead of time.

Camouflage and Concealment

A key part of survival in a non-permissive environment where there are people aiming to persecute you is camouflage and concealment. Camouflage is the technique used to ensure that you are disguised from would-be observers. It involves techniques to blend in with your surroundings. Concealment is the actual art of hiding something or preventing its whereabouts from being known. So, for instance, you can camouflage yourself and you can conceal equipment you are carrying on your person, for example, a weapon or food.

In some instances, you may have to make yourself known and reveal yourself without camouflage but still conceal something while being watched, such as a Bible in an urban area during the tribulation under martial law. This is called hiding in plain sight. In a way you are still camouflaged by blending in with your surroundings.

Take stock of your situation and the people and things in it. Does everyone wear black or gray instead of brown or green? Do people keep their hair long or short in that area? Are they smiling, or are their faces expressionless? Do they swing their arms when they walk, or do they hold both their hands behind their backs?

Camouflage and concealment do of course go hand in hand. When you are camouflaged, you are indeed keeping yourself concealed, along with that which is on your person.

A good way to stay camouflaged while surviving

in non-'permissive environments is to have a dedicated wardrobe for both urban and rural areas. For both areas you will want clothes that are drab in appearance and that do not stick out and make you a desirable target to a potential adversary.

For rural areas you may want to wear things that are a little closer to earth tones in color. For example, brown or khaki cargo pants worn with a green or brown shirt would be best for blending in with vegetation and dirt or mud.

Specific camouflaged clothing such as military or hunting uniforms or outfits are best for concealment, but unless you are trying to accomplish something specific, I wouldn't use them yet. The reason is that you don't want to be misidentified as a potential combatant in a situation that could potentially escalate. Always have a way out, and be prepared with an alibi. For footwear, I recommend earth tone hiking shoes or boots. Camouflage or other types of netting with green or brown earth tones can be worn as a poncho-type covering to help break up your outline. When worn over your clothing, it can be discarded if you need to switch to an urban setting.

For urban areas too, you should appear drab and uninteresting. Blue jeans and a gray shirt is probably your best bet. I don't recommend black, unless that's what everyone else is wearing, because black can stick out in the woods and may make you appear to be overcompensating in an urban setting. Black can also unknowingly express fanatical political or religious opinions that could get you in trouble. For footwear, hiking boots or dull-looking running shoes are best. Of course, your earth tone clothing and footwear for your rural attire has the potential to cross over to urban settings if need be. A cover shirt, such as a button-up dress shirt or flannel shirt, can also break up your outline in populated areas for purposes of concealment.

Making a Ghillie Suit

Because snipers have to rely so heavily on staying hidden in order to complete their missions, they have to take the time to consider how to blend in with their surroundings by creating what is known as a ghillie suit. All snipers are required to make one.

A ghillie suit is simply a suit that is worn in an attempt to break up your outline when you are trying to blend in with your surroundings. If you are trying to move in a manner so as not to be seen but you need to get to a certain area to see someone else's actions, you will depend on the use of this item.

Ghillie suits are not intended to be worn at all times as in certain nonrural areas they will appear to be out of the ordinary and will serve as a red flag to your adversary.

The best ghillie suits are made from old camouflage-pattern uniforms. On the knees up to the crotch of the pants, and on the elbows and stomach up to the chest of the uniform jacket, you will want to sew some thick canvas. The reason for this is that if you want to remain hidden, you will spend much time crawling around, and the canvas will keep your uniform from being torn. Green or brown canvas is the best color option to use for this.

On the other side of the uniform, cover the backs of the top and pants with brown or earth tone fishing netting. Attach the netting by sewing it to the material at every inch. Beware: this is a long process and will need to be completed long before you actually need the suit.

Also, be sure to find a camouflaged hat with a brim that goes all the way around. This also requires netting to be sewn on. Also, on the hat, top, and pants, be sure to sew three- to four-inch strands of 550 cord to the material about three to four inches apart all across the netting.

Once all the netting and 550 cord is sewn to the material, you are now ready to attach strands of burlap to the netting every two to three inches. The burlap, over time, will become ragged and frizzy in appearance. This is good because the inconsistent nature of this material will break up your outline while in wooded areas. Remember, with burlap or jute, less is oftentimes more.

The purpose of the 550 cord is so you can take natural vegetation from plants, by way of branches and leaves, and attach it to your ghillie suit for a more natural appearance. Keep in mind that when you have a lot of natural vegetation attached to your ghillie suit and you are walking around, you will simply look like plants walking around, which is out of the ordinary and alarming. Humans are natural predators; we know this because our eyes are on the front of our heads. To you this means that the easiest thing for humans to pick up on during the hunt is movement.

11

EQUIPMENT

Having the proper equipment available to you during a survival situation makes things so much easier. Good-quality equipment that will not break when you put it to use is a good investment in my book. The equipment you choose to use for survival should be tested regularly so that you have a good idea that it will last.

You should have your equipment set up and ready to go ahead of time so that you will not be scrambling around for things that you might need if there is an emergency and when time is of the essence. If you live in an area that is commonly affected by hurricane storms, you may already have a get-home bag or a bug-out bag on hand. If you don't have one of these set up, I highly recommend that you put one together. It doesn't take much. You can start off super simple and be better off than you were without it.

Just like with your survival pattern, when choosing the equipment that you will use, you should be thinking of food, water, shelter, fire, and signal when putting gear together. Of course you will need something to carry your equipment in. A comfortable and durable backpack of some sort is ideal.

> "As each one has received a gift, minister it to one another, as good stewards of the manifold grace of God" (1 Peter 4:10).

God has made each and every one of us unique and special. He has anointed us with many different blessings so we can use them to do good works and to glorify Him. As Christians waiting for Jesus to return, we must use our gifts for and with one another instead of sitting around and leading indolent lives. If God has given you a gift, then it is your responsibility to use it to do His will and not just sit on it.

> "All Scripture is given by inspiration of God, and is profitable for doctrine, for reproof, for correction, for instruction in righteousness, that the man of God may be complete, thoroughly equipped for every good work" (2 Timothy 3:16–17).

God has equipped us with the gift of all scripture to use for good works. Every question that anyone could ever have in this life can be answered through His Word and through prayer. One great thing about the Word of God being a gift is that it's the gift that keeps on giving.

> **The night is far spent, the day is at hand. Therefore let us cast off**

> **the works of darkness, and let us put on the armor of light. Let us walk properly, as in the day, not in revelry and drunkenness, not in lewdness and lust, not in strife and envy. But put on the Lord Jesus Christ, and make no provision for the flesh, to fulfill its lusts. (Romans 13:12-14)**

> **Do not be deceived, by beloved brethren. Every good gift and every perfect gift is from above, and comes from the Father of lights, with whom there is no variation or shadow of turning. (James 1:16-17)**

Night is the time when most people entertain themselves by drinking and being loud. When drunks and alcoholics get together in the party scene, they tend to be filled with the demonic spirit of lust and begin to act sexually offensive toward one another. As the night progresses and people have more to drink than they should, they begin to stumble around and yell angrily at one another until eventually conflict breaks out, usually over nothing important.

As sober-minded Christians, it's our job to put on the armor of God, who is the Father of Lights. Because we are children of God, we are the light of the world. We should act accordingly by putting on His armor and not stumbling around in a drunken stupor.

Now that we are in the latter days and the tribulation is on the horizon, the devil wants us to leave our armor at home and take a luxury cruise of drunkenness and sexual temptation. He is the captain of "the boat of lies," and he wants to eventually leave us in open waters to fight with one another. The father of lies will try to lure you in by making it seem like harmless and desirable fun. He wants us to be caught with our guard down.

Think of a boat leaving a dock. When you unfasten a boat line so that the boat can depart the port, it's called "casting off." Rather than setting sail with the works of darkness, stay on dry land, where you can walk properly on more stable ground. In the end, God will sink the boat and the captain will go down with it. All of His people with be on solid, dry land sowing His good seeds and casting out the bad ones, waiting for His return.

> **Finally, my brethren, be strong in the Lord and in the power of His might. Put on the whole armor of God, that you may be able to stand against the wiles of the devil. For we do not wrestle against flesh and blood, but against principalities, against powers, against the rulers of the darkness of this age, against spiritual hosts of wickedness in the heavenly places. Therefore take up the whole armor of God, that you may be able to withstand in the evil day, and having done all, to stand. (Ephesians 6:10–13)**

Without the armor of God, we are powerless against the devil because his power is greater than our flesh. There are angelic and demonic powers and principalities that are warring over our souls every day of our lives. They are around us. We cannot always see them, but they are there. The rulers of darkness, spiritual hosts of wickedness, are in heavenly places including the earth, but they can never come close to the third and highest level of heaven, which is where God's throne is. We are to wear this armor so that on the day when these evil ones bring a full assault on our lives, we will be able to withstand and defeat them.

> **Stand therefore, having girded your waist with truth, having put on the breastplate of righteousness, and having shod your feet with the preparation of the gospel of peace; above all, taking the shield of faith with which you will be able to quench all the fiery darts of the wicked one. And take the helmet of salvation, and the sword of the Spirit, which is the word of God; praying always with all prayer and supplication in the Spirit, being watchful to this end with all perseverance and supplication for all the saints—and for me, that utterance may be given to me, that I may open my mouth boldly to make known the mystery of the gospel, for which I am an ambassador in chains; that in it I may speak boldly, as I ought to speak. (Ephesians 6:14-20)**

The first piece of armor mentioned is the truth, which holds all the other pieces of the armor together. Next is the breastplate of righteousness.

Because of the truth of Jesus Christ, we become righteous in our hearts and should never let anything evil trick us into believing otherwise.

When your feet are shod with the preparation of the gospel of peace, you are always ready to be on the move at a moment's notice to complete the will of God by telling others about the peace that Jesus brings to our lives.

The shield of faith is one of the most important pieces of armor because it is your first line of defense during an attack from the enemy.

When you wear the helmet of salvation, you are protecting the sound mind of Jesus that God gave you, so you will be able to focus on the Word of God with obedience.

When you set out to spread the gospel and tell others about Jesus Christ, you will need the Spirit of God, which comes from the Word of God. Your faith will allow you to block any negative accusations that come your way, and the Word of God will be like a sword that thrusts a counterattack that delivers the death blow.

Winning these spiritual battles is paramount for all Christians to be able to harvest souls. However, without the *full* armor of God, you allow yourself to be open to attack as each piece goes hand in hand with the others. By picking up your cross daily and putting on the full armor of God, you have absolutely no chance of losing any spiritual battle. Thank God that He has provided us with all the necessary tools and equipment to get the job done.

Bug-Out Bag

A bug-out bag, also known as a start-over bag, holds the items necessary for your survival. You should also have a smaller bag or fanny pack within the bug-out bag with your most basic needs for survival in case you need to ditch the main pack for the sake of speed and outrunning an adversary.

When planning a bug-out bag or BOB for a family, many decisions must be made in terms of needs versus wants. With children, it's hard to make cuts because they rely so heavily on being taken care of.

When children are old enough, they should be able to carry a small backpack with just their basic needs such as clothing, a toothbrush, water, a snack, a blanket or sleeping bag, an emergency poncho, and a comfort item such as a toy or stuffed animal. These items will sustain them for a small period of time in case they get separated from you. Think of everything that you would pack for your kids if they were going to spend the night at Grandma's house. It will also help the child remain proactive and keep his or her morale up during a disaster or an emergency if he or she has a small amount of responsibility to be in charge of.

For adults with no kids, it's a little bit easier because you can pack lighter, and you are able to manage with a higher level of discomfort than families with small children.

Do you think packing a BOB is perhaps a little overzealous? Think of all the disasters that could force a person out of their home: tornado, hurricane, earthquake, wildfire, flooding, and even civil unrest. Can you guarantee that these things will never happen to you in your lifetime? Me neither.

Many situations require that you have items

on hand so you are able to leave a situation for your own survival. In the event that you have to leave your home or town to get yourself and your family out of harm's way, you should take a bug-out bag or BOB.

It is doctrine in most cases that one should prepare for such a disaster by having a bug-out bag ready that holds supplies that will last for seventy-two hours. I believe that three to five days is a good start, but the contents of your bag should allow you to sustain yourself for an extended period of time while on the move to a better location that may present better options.

You should have a resupply point that only you and other members of your party know about. Plan routes with contingencies.

Bugging out is often considered more exciting than bugging in. I'm not sure why, although people are more likely to bug in during cold and wet conditions.

Bugging out is the last resort. Chances are that you have already been bugging in, and things have gotten so bad that you have to leave your dwelling. Chances are, it's dangerous outside your home, especially when you feel enough pressure that you're willing to evacuate your home with your family.

Apart from bugging out, we will addressed the need to get home first. Just as a fighter pilot has an ejection seat in the event that his or her aircraft is unrecoverable and destined to crash, you should have a bailout plan.

Make a list of the gear you will pack in your bug-out bag. The bag itself should be a quality bag between fifty and eighty liters in size for the intent of not coming back home. The following

is a suggested list of gear that I believe is a good baseline. Feel free to add or take away as you see fit:
- **Bible**—This should be the number one item on your list!

Food
- Long-term-storage food
- Protein bars
- Beef jerky
- Jar of peanuts or peanut butter

Water
- Water bottle
- Water filter bottle
- Iodine drops
- Canteen cup to boil water in

Shelter
- Reflective tarp for insulation
- Poncho/tarp and tent stakes
- Sleeping bag

Fire
- Lighter
- Flint and steel
- Matches

Signal
- Orange bandanna
- Blaze-orange reflective vest
- Chem lights
- Pen flares
- Cell phone and charger
- Two-way radios

First Aid
- First aid kit
  - Gauze, ACE bandage, tourniquet, scissors, medical tape, rubber gloves, sterile alcohol wipes, medical book for referencing

Equipment
- Toiletries
  - TP, soap, towel, toothbrush, toothpaste, hand wipes, hand sanitizer
- Good pair of hiking shoes or boots
- Change of clothes
  - Pants
  - Thin-layer insulation pants
  - Running shorts
  - T-shirt
  - Socks
  - Underwear
  - Long-sleeve T-shirt / thin-layer long-sleeve
- Watch cap
- Mosquito net for head
- Insulated jacket lining
- Windbreaker jacket
- Rain jacket
- 550 cord (50 ft.)
- Bungee cord (2)
- Boonie hat
- Work gloves
- Duct tape
- Zip ties
- Pocketknife
- Minimalist survival kit

- o Lighter, matches, fishing lines, hooks, sinkers, bobbers, small knife, small reflective poncho, aluminum foil
- Extra pistol magazines, magazine holders, pistol holster
- Hatchet
- Extra batteries
- Trash bags
- Large knife or hatchet and sharpener
- Entrenching tool
- Quality compass
- Camouflage clothing or netting

550 Cord Bootlaces

Many people wear survival bracelets made of paracord. Another technique that I like is substituting anything that functions like string such as bootlaces. When using 550 cord as bootlaces, make sure that you burn the ends so that the individual strands do not unravel.

Get-Home Bag

Pack items that you wish to have on hand and available for use to get home in case of an emergency. Choose a quality bag between thirty and fifty liters in size. Leave it in your car or next to your office desk. Include the following items:

- Bible
- Snack bars
- Water filter bottle
- Water bottle
- Poncho
- Small sleeping bag
- Lighter, matches, flint, and steel

- Thin-layer change of clothes:
  - Pants, shirt, underwear, socks, shoes
- Windbreaker jacket
- Emergency poncho
- Ball cap
- Knife
- Bungee cord
- Multitool
- Canteen cup
- 550 cord
- Snack bars
- Extra pistol magazine
- Small spade or shovel
- Work gloves
- Bandanna
- Small minimalist survival kit
  - Lighter, matches, fishing lines, hooks, sinkers, bobbers, small knife, small reflective poncho, aluminum foil

Your fanny pack that you keep inside either of these two bags should contain the bare minimum gear you need for survival. As a mobile piece of gear, it should also be carried with you on your person if the situation dictates, such as a trip to the beach, a trip to the park, or a light hike on a trail.

Minimalist Survival Kit:
- Lighter, matches, fishing lines, hooks, sinkers, bobbers, small knife, small reflective poncho, aluminum foil
- Survival water filter straw
- ID cards and passports—situation dependent
- USB flash drive

- Copy of ID cards and passports
- Copy of family photo
- Copy of birth certificates
- Anything else you want a copy of

Every day carry items or EDC are the things that you take with you in your day-to-day life to support the most probable everyday events that you encounter. In addition, you should be prepared for other things to take place, such as defending yourself in a life-or-death situation against a person with malicious intent to harm or kill you.

Besides the bags you carry for different situations, your EDC supplies you at a moment's notice with the bare minimum required to survive no matter where you are. Although you can't always have all these items in restricted areas such as airports, God gave you the ability to think outside the box and to adapt and improvise.

- ▶ Wallet
- ▶ Keys
- ▶ Watch
- ▶ Sunglasses
- ▶ Phone
- ▶ Pocketknife
- ▶ Flashlight
- ▶ Self-defense mechanism (usually one of the below)—
    - o Pepper spray
    - o Taser
    - o Compact or subcompact pistol
    - o Extra magazine

12

BE PREPARED

Some Christians may argue that if you are truly a Christian, then you should have faith that God will provide for you in the end times and rapture you before the tribulation. Some say that preparing for the end days is showing a lack of trust in God that He will provide for you. Do these same Christians have jumper cables in their cars, or a generator for when the power goes out, or life insurance for their families when they die? How about a 401(k) or other types of savings accounts? Do they let their kids go off with strangers? No, because God gave us a sound mind.

Jesus never said that being a Christian would be easy. I don't believe that Jesus gave us the signs of the end times just so we would sit around and wait for things to happen to us. I believe that we do have a discipleship that entails a mission from God to save our fellow people.

If we are not to prepare for battle, then why should we study the Word of God, which is a sword? Why put on the armor of God to do battle? God put us here to do His will on earth as it is in heaven and to put those spiritual tools to work, not just stand around like ostriches with our heads buried in the sand.

> **He who tills his land will have plenty of bread, but he who follows frivolity will have poverty enough! (Proverbs 28:19)**

> **For you yourselves know perfectly that the day of the Lord so comes as a thief in the night. For when they say, "Peace and safety!" then sudden destruction comes upon them, as labor pains upon a pregnant woman. And they shall not escape. But you, brethren, are not in darkness, so that this Day should overtake you as a thief. (1 Thessalonians 5:2–4)**

God wants His people to be prepared and not be caught off guard. When the Antichrist arrives, those who have studied the Word of God will have discernment and will not fall for the lies about the period of peace and safety before the destruction of the temple. Christians will be ready when the dragon defiles the temple.

Jesus told us about the signs of the end times in Matthew 24 so that we would be prepared. In knowing that we have hard times ahead of us and that faith without works is dead, it's easy enough to comprehend that if you till the land, you will have bread. And those who are consumed with things that lack any real importance, let alone spiritual importance, will be left in poverty.

Satan sends his demons to distract you into being consumed with things that will derail you from your mission. God, however, sends His angels to war against the demons of distraction, especially to those who are obedient in prayer.

> **There is desirable treasure,
> And oil in the dwelling of the wise,
> But a foolish man squanders it.**
>
> **—Proverbs 21:20**

> **Then one from the crowd said to Him, "Teacher, tell my brother to divide the inheritance with me."**
>
> **But He said to him, "Man, who made Me a judge or an arbitrator over you?" And He said to them, "Take heed and beware of covetousness, for one's life does not consist in the abundance of the things he possesses."**
>
> **Then He spoke a parable to them, saying: "The ground of a certain rich man yielded plentifully. And he thought within himself, saying, 'What shall I do, since I have no room to store my crops?' So he said, 'I will do this: I will pull down my barns and build greater, and there I will store all my crops and my goods. And I will say to my soul, "Soul, you have many goods laid up for many years; take your ease; eat, drink, and be merry."' But God said to him, 'Fool! This night**

> your soul will be required of you; then whose will those things be which you have provided?'
>
> "So is he who lays up treasure for himself, and is not rich toward God." (Luke 12:13-21)

You may be familiar with the children's story of the ants and the grasshopper. The wise ants spent all summer working hard to store up food for the winter so they would have plenty to live off of. The grasshopper spent all summer just foolishly eating as he went along at his leisure. When winter arrived, the grasshopper eventually resorted to begging the ants for food to survive.

The man from Jesus's story obtained his wealth legally. But the man sinned because he saved up his wealth with the intention of using it to spend the rest of his life taking it easy, not with the intention of doing God's will. When you die, it won't matter how much you have stored up on earth if you haven't used it to do God's will. So, the man from the crowd who wanted his brother to divide the inheritance should have been more worried about the inheritance that is promised by God in heaven.

As Christians, while we make our preparations, we need to ensure that we are sharing our inheritance with our brothers and sisters willingly. The things that we have stored up for troubled times will do us no good when we stand before God's throne if we did not feed others when they are hungry or give them water when they are thirsty. Your treasures should be stored in heaven (Matthew 6:19-20).

> "But if anyone does not provide for his own, and especially for those of his household, he has denied the faith and is worse than an unbeliever" (1 Timothy 5:8).

As head of household or even a member of any household, you are with the family God chose for you to be a part of. You are a part of that family so you can be a blessing to them as a believer in Christ. Your presence in your household should let the light of Jesus shine.

In the end of times when other families will turn each other in to be put to death, Christian families should work with other Christian families to ensure a strong congregation of children of God to do His will.

> "A prudent man foresees evil and hides himself, but the simple pass on and are punished" (Proverbs 22:3).

Christians should take heed because God has provided us with revelation in His Word. *Revelation* literally means the revealing of something. Throughout the entire Bible, scripture contains prophecies that lead to the last days and point to Jesus as the Messiah and God's final judgment on earth. Because we have received prophecy and because we have faith, we also have prudence. We will not fall for the lies of the Antichrist and his false prophet during the end times. Those who lack in faith and knowledge will take the mark of the beast and will be punished with the fullness of God's wrath along with the devil.

> "The horse is prepared for the day of battle, but deliverance is of the Lord" (Proverbs 21:31).

As we prepared for troubled times and tribulation, we should remember that it's not for our benefit. Your soul was bought and paid for by the blood of Jesus Christ; it doesn't belong to you! Your house, your body, and all your belongings should be used to glorify the victory that belongs to God.

One of the few things that sets rangers apart from all other light infantry units is their ability to plan and prepare for situations while in training before these things are encountered in a real-world scenario. The other side of this military distinction is the ability to improvise, adapt, and overcome the situations that haven't been trained for. Trying new things that require you to perform your task outside of your comfort level or in an uncommon manner is the best way to increase your chances of success during abnormal circumstances.

Knowing how to survive by living off in the land with the absolute bare minimum is an invaluable skill set. If you are reading *Millennial Ranger*, it is because you already have the determination to survive in harsh situations should you be required to do so. The purpose of the section discussing how to prepare isn't to tell you what to do and what not to do but to simply open your mind to get you thinking outside the box. You may already have a plan in effect, but you might have overlooked a few possibilities. Again, the purpose of this isn't to tell you that I'm right and you're wrong.

My advice is to go on, if possible, thriving without having to put up a struggle by venturing out to find resources. Food shortages at the supermarket could happen instantaneously when hurricane weather or other natural disasters approach. When the power goes out, how will you stay hydrated? How will you bathe to maintain your hygiene? If a disaster breeds lawlessness in your community, how will you stop armed intruders from entering your home and taking from you and your family what's rightfully yours? Don't think this could happen? Take a look at the situations that developed in the wake of Hurricane Katrina in Louisiana. You need to be prepared to ensure your own safety and survivability and that of your loved ones and possibly other members of your community.

Preparing for the worst and hoping for the best is fast becoming the more normal way of life among average American citizens. In some parts of the world outside the United States, people are already facing horrific circumstances that force them to function and survive outside the typical comfort zone of normal human living.

Many people around the country have many different views and ideas on survival preparations or prepping. One of the biggest reasons why people choose not to prepare for catastrophic events is that they are worried about all the naysayers in their society. Nobody wants to be the crazy person who is waiting for the world to end while the neighbors talk about them behind their back. I get it: a single catastrophic event causing human extinction more than likely won't happen in the next thirty seconds as you are in the middle of reading *Millennial Ranger*. Consider one thing, though: Noah built an ark over a long period of time in the middle of the desert, and no one listened to his warning he received from God. In fact, he was surrounded by scoffers.

How does this apply to you and me? Well, if you are a Christian and a student of the Bible, you are familiar with the Second Coming of Jesus Christ promised in God's Word. This Second Coming of Christ involves a great tribulation period in that all people must endure before the Christians are raptured. Although some Christians believe that the rapture will happen before the tribulation period, I believe that the Bible tells us that the rapture will happen after the seven-year tribulation.

In the book of Revelation, we see that during the tribulation there are some things that are going to put people well outside their comfort zones, such as war and famine, as discussed earlier. Imagine a United States with war and famine on our front doorstep. War and famine can bring on just about anything and everything that people will have to overcome in order to survive. This isn't going to *maybe* happen; the Bible says that this *will* happen—and many, including me, believe it will happen sooner rather than later and in our lifetime.

Prepping for survival during the end times is to ensure that you have all elements of a survival pattern in ample supply and ready to be used at a moment's notice in the event of a catastrophic event. Being prepped also consists of the ability and know-how to improvise survival as a backup plan when you are left with nothing but your own devices. The more you practice survival, the more you are conditioning yourself to be an outside-the-box thinker willing to improvise in order to adapt to situations where you may no longer have your prepared resources available to you.

The best way to become a better prepper is by researching different techniques with other people who are like-minded in terms of survival. You'll probably find that along the way you are prone to harvest souls before anything even happens when you tell other people why you are making preparations.

People are prepping for certain things such as economic collapse, natural disasters, power grid failure, war, and civil unrest. These individual things that people choose to prepare for are mere by-products of the one thing the Bible tells us about, namely, the end of times and the seven-year tribulation. *All* these inevitable events should be considered, not just one or two! I believe that an individual who is aspiring to prepare for survival is better off getting ready for any type of situation and not just one extreme situation. You are way better off covering all aspects, rather than just leaning toward one end of the spectrum.

Many were astonished when the CDC website had preparation tips for how to prepare for a zombie apocalypse. I think this was a great idea considering the current following of the zombie genre by the younger generations. The whole idea makes a lot of sense considering that if you are prepared for the proverbial "zombie apocalypse," you will be prepared for any major disaster. With this in mind, you may want to have your own smallholding setup just as a hobby to start off with. The more you are used to living off the grid before a crisis occurs, the better off you will be once events unfold that cause the grid to go down unexpectedly.

Remember, in survival and preparing to survive, knowledge is key. You will walk a fine line between what you and others may consider kosher while networking ideas and what may be a breach of your personal security by leaking too much information that could make you a target for people who want what you have. So be cautious during your preparations! Also, ensure that you are not a target for identity theft either!

There are a great many hypotheticals and what-ifs that people generally tend to obsess about, ultimately leading them to become tied up in one extreme topic. This type of tunnel vision will not allow an individual to be well-rounded and flexible, as more than likely more will be required in many situations. When I was young, the Boy Scouts taught me to always be prepared. As a ranger, I learned from my unit's American heritage that Major Robert Rogers told his men, "Don't forget nothing," as rule number one of his standing orders. It is this type of attention to detail that could mean the difference between life and death when considering your preparations for your survival in this already uncertain world.

Contrary to popular belief, not all the answers relating to techniques of preparing for survival in the physical world can be found in just one book. However, all things related to spiritual survival can be found in one book, which is the Word of God. Although any bit of information that you can hold on to is invaluable, you will never be a true master of prepping or survival just by reading any one article.

It seemingly takes a great deal of time and life events to acquire the knowledge required to properly prepare for just about anything. Knowledge is the first step, and practicing and applying your new skills are the next and final steps. You should always seek to improve your knowledge and skills; never get too comfortable and become lazy. Your greatest enemy is complacency, and complacency kills.

Do not be discouraged, as you may feel that you are too late to the game and already behind the power curve. You don't need all the high-speed gear that the self-proclaimed professionals use. Start small with your preparations and work your way up, starting with something simple such as food and water. From there, keep improving and adding other things. Remember that any preparation is better than no preparation at all.

As you move from one area to the next in your preparations, cycle around to adding to all the elements that make up your plan. Fix the missing or broken links in your chain mail as you put it together. Take your time, and think about what you're doing; slow is smooth, and smooth is fast. The only plan that is perfect is God's plan. Prepare your soul constantly. Pray often, and never stop praying, not even when you feel that you are alone. Remember, God will never abandon you! After you have done your part, trust that God will take care of the rest.

I'm planning on being prepared for the promised tribulation period that Jesus tells us will happen in the book of Matthew 24. In the book of Revelation, we receive an even more severe understanding of just how horrible the tribulation will be. If you are prepared for Christ's return, then you will truly be prepared for something as simple as survival. You will only be able to purchase everyday items such as food, water, clothing, and even electricity if you receive the mark of the beast. As far as I am concerned, at that point the grid will mean nothing and might as well be gone anyway. This is why preparing your soul is an absolute top priority. If you take the mark of the beast for a meal today, you will be spending the rest of eternity in hell!

God loves you! God loves you so much that He gave His only Son to free the world from death through His grace. Jesus has saved you from sin. God loves you so much that He also gave us all a heads-up that Jesus will return, and He wants us to be ready because He has sent you His Word found in the Bible, which is the ultimate survival manual.

Food

There are several different methods of preparing food for long-term storage. Most of the methods have been in use since the pioneer days of the parts of North America that became the United States. For most average American citizens, storing food means going to the grocery store and buying a bunch of canned foods off the shelves. There is nothing wrong this method. Canned foods can last for several years and are easy to store in tight spaces. This is fine as long as you store the food ahead of time. Most people wait until they are notified that a bad storm is heading their way before they rush to the stores. A lot of the time people show up to these stores only to find that the shelves have been cleaned out and left empty. Imagine if you were one of these people and you and your family were really counting on the canned food from the store; you would return home to some very disappointed people.

Buying and storing canned foods from the grocery store isn't necessarily a bad idea; any preparations you make is better than no preparation at all. If you go this route and/or if this is your primary source of emergency food storage, just keep in mind that you will want to continuously rotate the cans, eating the older food and buying new food to keep your supply fresh. It would be a shame to have a large amount of canned foods on standby only to find that they are all out of date when you really need them. A good technique is to figure out how many canned foods you eat in a year, then figure out how many years it will take for each type of food to expire, and then adjust from there, rotating the food to keep your supplies fresh. It may also help to have a nearby chart of your canned food inventory to help you keep track. Another reassuring factor is that studies have shown that canned foods can still be consumed awhile after their expiration date. I imagine that this is more the case when the cans are stored in cool places. Eat expired foods at your own risk.

If you were planning on just roughing it for about a week or so, you may get by with just canned goods. But what happens when the approaching disaster is more than just a storm passing through? What if something so terrible were to happen that would cause store shelves to remain empty for very long periods of time?

Eventually, days turn into weeks, weeks turn into months, and when things are really bad, months turn into years. By now your whole world is upside down. The authorities say help is on the way, but that is uncertain at best. It's no use going to the stores that once had food on the shelves. Those shelves are now riddled with garbage and random bits of debris, and the stores are inhabited by unreceptive squatters seeking shelter, looking for any opportunity to better their current situation, even if it means they must harm others. At this point you are confined to only one option: relying on a government that has turned cold and imbalanced in the midst of the detrition of your society.

There are many options available to prevent you from being caught unprepared. All these options have their pros and cons. Some methods require more work than others. It's up to you to come up with the best plan possible to cater to your needs and those of your loved ones. Your best bet is to consider all the options applicable to your needs and use them in conjunction with each other.

The quickest and easiest—and somewhat costly—method to ensure you have an ample supply of food for any disaster is to buy freeze-dried foods. I say this is the most expensive method because usually one buys this type of item in large quantities. Realistically, this method is actually cheaper per serving compared to buying canned food from the grocery store (about thirty cents per serving).

This type of food is amazing because, depending on where you get it from, it can be stored from ten to twenty years depending on how you store it. Another great benefit of freeze-dried food is that once you purchase it, that's it—all you must do is add some hot water and you are ready to feed yourself and your family. Although storing military MREs (meals ready to eat) is not a bad option either, the freeze-dried foods will last longer, and they taste better too.

You will be able to store enough food that will last years for yourself and your family as long as you are willing to buy what you need in bulk. If you do not have the financial means to buy in large bulk, you can still purchase smaller containers and over time have nice store set up. Keep in mind that you do not want to have a high-level profile and that it's best to conceal your food store as best as you can to prevent becoming a future target to those who would do anything to keep from starving.

Canning food is another common and very effective option for storing food. This method of food storage requires time and experience as it is an art. The secret to canning food is knowing what recipes to use for which type of food you want to can. After that, the process of preparing the food is similar for all fruits and vegetables.

Dehydrating foods is another good way to prolong the shelf life of foods that you don't need to use right away. It is inexpensive and very effective.

Farming and growing crops is the best way to constantly ensure that you have a steady supply of food to consume and prepare for storage. Chickens and their eggs are a great source of protein. Goats have highly nutritious milk. Both animals are grazing animals, so the bigger the yard you have, the more goats and chickens you can have.

Water

More important than food, water is an absolute must if you are preparing for surviving off the grid. The longest humans can go without water is three days. You could have truckloads of food, but without water it would all be worthless. If you fail to have water stored for survival, then you are done.

For most people, water is obviously important for drinking, cooking, and bathing. We use it every day. However, the average American has grown quite accustomed to simply turning a knob or opening a valve to obtain water.

It is easy to forget just how important it is to have water in our lives until it suddenly gets taken away. When severe weather is upon us and the power goes out, a very humbling and sober thought enters our brains when we remember that access to water is a privilege and not a right. When you have no source on standby and there is no water to be had because the local supermarket is fresh out, you and your family will be very disappointed. For those of us who have been in this situation before, we know better now. If there is a threatening storm on its way toward our area, one of the first things we do is fill up buckets, sinks, and bathtubs with water because by the time we get to the store, it's already gone. Also, by the time the power goes out for whatever reason, we are too late.

One thing you can do to make life a little easier during these times is to frequently buy water and use store-bought water on a regular basis. This will allow you the opportunity to have a constant water supply as you will use it before it goes bad and you rotate in new water to replace the old.

So, rotating water bottles and filling up bathtubs may be your solution for when you expect the power to go out because of a storm, but what if you are not expecting anything to happen because you have not been warned properly? Suddenly you and your family are left without. Those water bottles won't last forever, and once again you will be directed to the local market, caught up in a very sad situation much to your dismay.

You can prevent such a distressing event from happening in your life by having a large enough container on standby to hold even more water, in addition to the rotated bottles of store-bought water and filled-up bathtubs.

Water storage tanks come in several different shapes and sizes coming from several different manufacturers that are in fact FDA (Food and Drug Administration) approved for holding water for human consumption. What the term "FDA approved" means when applied to tanks is that you do not have to worry about the materials used to construct the container in which you plan to store your drinking water being contaminated.

One thing to consider when using large water containers is that you want to clean them out thoroughly whether they are brand new or used. This will kill germs that may have been introduced during the shipping and handling process. Also, cleaning the containers will get rid of any debris along with any odors of new plastic.

Remember that when filling up your container intended for holding drinking water, you should use a food-grade hose rather than a regular garden hose to reduce the risk of lead settling in the barrel/container/tank over time.

Do not store barrels on cement surfaces because this can cause a chemical reaction that causes leakage. Instead, store the container on a wooden platform such as a pallet or plywood. Keep your container slightly elevated above ground level in order to use gravity to your advantage in aiding with water flow. It's okay to have your wooden platform on top of a row of cinder blocks as long as everything rests steadily.

The water inside the storage container needs to be treated much like water in a survival situation. Do not use bleach, because it can create stomach ulcers and cause diarrhea. Chlorine is better for storage, and it can be filtered out later specifically for drinking.

There are several different methods for filtrating water. The makeshift water filter you would use in a survival situation is a good option for filtering, only now you have more reliable materials available to construct a filter ahead of time. Also, you have the time to test the effectiveness of your homemade water filter so that you may become more proficient at constructing more filters over time.

In addition to your homemade water filters, there are several different types of commercially manufactured filters you can use. These filters are proven to be very effective at filtering out debris, bacteria, and even nuclear waste. These filters are costly and do expire in time with enough use. I like to think that when it comes to the safety of my drinking water, you get what you pay for; plus, you can always stock up on filters and replace the old ones as needed.

So now that you have your store-bought water rotation plan, your emergency bathtub plan, and your large water storage with filter plan, you should be all set, right? Well, not completely. In the event of a storm, you should be good with these precautions. But what if the storm is so severe that the power is down for longer than you expected? If you are prepared for the grid to go down and you have a year's supply of water that you've carefully calculated for yourself and your family, what will you do after, I don't know, a year later when the power is still down and there is still no grid? Eventually you will need to replenish your water store as it will not last forever.

Some people may already be fortunate enough to live on a well or are able to create one at the location where they live. You may also be fortunate enough to live by a natural freshwater source like a stream or a lake. If you don't, you might want to move to a piece of land where you can achieve this. Moving is always an option if you are serious enough, but obviously this is not an option for everyone, especially on a tight budget with a low income. Don't worry; even though you don't have enough money to buy a piece of land with the perfect freshwater source, you are still in luck. We still have the rain that God gives us. Harvesting rain seems like the best option for ensuring a stable supply of water for storage. Of course the location of your homestead may come in to play when determining the actual value of this method.

Even if you are not in the middle of a catastrophic event, harvesting rain in barrels is an efficient and frugal way to water your lawn or your modest vegetable garden without having to increase your water bill. Setting up a system like this will pay for itself over time.

There are many different setups you can use to harvest rain. All methods are ideally the same in concept. Funnel all the water from the rooftop of your house through a gutter system. This system will go through a series of filters leading down to the top of the barrel or barrels. Most likely the barrel will have a spigot toward the bottom. It is also likely that you will construct an elevated platform to allow gravity to push the water out of the spigot and possibly through a connected hose. You can also use piping systems to connect multiple barrels in one system side by side, allowing you to store and use as much water as you need. Remember, the water you harvest from the rain must be treated if you wish to drink it, cook with it, or bathe in it. You should keep the water as filtered as possible and sealed off so mosquitoes and other bugs will not breed in your barrels.

So now you have a variety of methods to use that escalate in priority as the situation may dictate or even go from bad to worse. Maintaining a constant supply of water is a must for consumption and use for yourself, your family, your livestock, and your pets. You have a method for maintaining crops as well. Your imagination is the limit. You will find ways to construct contingency systems over time.

Bugging In

At your house or a known point that can be used as a stronghold or dwelling against any disaster, bugging in is usually the preferred method before bugging out ever takes place. Think about it: does it really make sense to be running around crazily during a disaster just because other people are running around crazily?

To me, I think of a bug-in location as your home and how you would set it up if your house were to be a homestead. Try not to look at it as a bug-in site where you must be barricaded in to stay safe. Although I personally think that bunkers have their place, you can set up your home to be bug-in-worthy without constructing a bunker just yet.

Most people don't have the luxury of just quitting their jobs and moving out in the middle of nowhere to set up a homestead. That's no problem. Many people have the ability to grow urban gardens where they currently live in residential neighborhoods. Livestock may be an issue. Another option may be to set up a plan with your network of family members and friends who may live farther outside of town and away from the coast.

Consider this: you or your spouse is at work while the other one of you is running around doing errands. Your child or children are at school, perhaps on the opposite end of town. In the event of an emergency or catastrophic event that may require evacuation, how will you get your family to safety? You will need to have a plan in effect for your family ahead of time. You may have to utilize bug-out methods or make your way back home in order to bug in. Have a plan with other members of your family that consists of routes and rally points in case all members are initially separated in the event of a disaster.

Your home may not be good enough, so you may need a secondary location that you can get to. Your best course of action may have to be bugging out before you can bug in, for example, in the event of a hurricane or other type of storm.

When the power goes out, one of the first things that people do as soon as they get the chance is to fire up the generator to try to establish some semblance of normalcy and return to how things were before the lights stopped working. The problem with generators is that they make a lot of noise, which sparks the interest of would-be intruders running amok looking to take advantage of the situation. Another option is a solar-powered fuel-less generator with a space heater. A fuel-less generator makes no sound and is safe to keep inside your dwelling. You want your bug-in location to be as unassuming as possible. If you are going to run gas-powered generators, make sure that you keep an eye out for suspicious activity in your neighborhood. Keep track by making a range card and sector sketches.

Just like a fire in the wilderness, a fire in your fireplace can give off smoke and give away your position as a target indicator for your enemy or looters. You should have multiple ways to keep your home warm and use your better judgment when it comes to utilizing each method based on the situation.

Health and Hygiene

One of the most important things that you can do in your life, whether preparing or not, is to maintain good health. The bad habits that you engage in today will affect your way of life tomorrow. Maintaining good health includes such things as proper eating, sleeping, and exercising, and practicing good spiritual habits such as praying.

In the military, we refer to PT (physical training) as preventative maintenance. Lifting weights, running, stretching, and just all around maintaining an active lifestyle is essential to preventing injuries in your day-to-day life. One important thing to remember is not to overdo it when exercising. Yes, it is good to challenge yourself, but not to the point that you are hurting or injuring yourself. If you are not used to lifting weights, start off with push-ups instead of bench press. Simple exercises such as push-ups, sit-ups, pull-ups, and running are great even for the most experienced gym enthusiasts.

Have you ever heard the direction, "Eat to live; don't live to eat"? Just because something tastes good doesn't mean it is good for you. Remember, your body is a temple, and your life doesn't belong to you anymore; it was bought and paid for by the blood of Jesus Christ. It is important to make sure that you maintain a healthy level of cholesterol today so that if it's slim pickings in the chow line, you will be ahead of the game. You don't want to start the tribulation period with your health already on the decline. I'm not saying that you have to stick to a strictly regimented diet plan; just make healthy decisions now before it becomes a problem.

Now is the time to quit smoking! Your lungs have the ability to heal themselves; you just need to give them that chance. Smoking and the use of chewing tobacco restricts your blood flow, which in turn could slow down any healing process should you become injured. Of course the use of cigarettes and chewing tobacco can cause cancer as well.

Now is the time to quit drinking alcohol! Alcohol is one of the worst things that you can put in your body if you want to build muscle and be on the right track to a healthier lifestyle. Alcohol will also impair your physical control and your ability to make rational decisions. In the old spaghetti westerns, the protagonist would sometimes take a shot of whiskey before engaging in an action-packed shootout. In the real world, consuming alcohol before a task such as driving a car, let alone a gun battle, is dangerous and can put the lives of nearby people in mortal danger. Remember, alcohol is also poison to your body.

Now is the time to quit using drugs! Nothing good can come of taking drugs on a regular basis, even if they're legal. If you had some sort of pain in the past and you became hooked on pain medication, that is the work of the devil. Satan wants you to think that you need these sort of things in your life and that God is not enough to take them away. You need to pray for healing and rebuke the evil spirit of addiction. If this is something that you are struggling with, you can seek help from members of your church or family and ask them to strengthen you through prayer. You are already healed—and God always answers prayers!

Sleep. All living creatures require sleep to reenergize and grow. Even sharks, which once were believed never to sleep, require rest. You should have at least seven to eight hours of sleep each night to maintain good health. You may be wondering if you should try to get used to no sleep in case you are put in a situation that calls for staying awake. I'm here to tell you that I have been put in such a situation and that you don't ever technically get used to it. You may be able to deal with it—the human will is an amazing thing—but sleep deprivation is never a good thing. Even people who don't sleep on a regular basis suffer from not getting enough rest. Another good thing to do is to pray before sleep. During sleep is when you receive visions and revelations from the Holy Spirit (Numbers 12:6).

Maintaining good hygiene can directly affect your health. If you are in a bug-in situation and you don't have a plan for trash or your waste, that filth will become a harbor for bacteria and diseases. If you don't have a way to take showers and brush your teeth, you should make a plan for that as well. You can use goat's milk as the main ingredient to make your own soap. Good hygiene also greatly contributes to morale, which is a huge factor in survival. Washing your dishes and clothes will be a challenge, but it is something that must be done as well.

I've seen firsthand what Third World countries look like when there is no effective waste plan in effect. I can tell you that the stench reeks at unbearable levels, especially in urban areas. When there is no plumbing and there is nowhere to do one's business, people tend to just throw their waste in the streets. Trash blows around on the sidewalks of these cities like it's a natural part of the scenery. I would go so far to say that there are some major cities in the United States that are only a step and a half away from this type of situation.

A good technique and a timeless classic for disposing of human waste is the use of an outhouse. The wooden shedlike structure should be constructed far enough away from your home that you don't have to smell it all the time. Underneath the built-in seat should be a metal bucket of some sort to trap the fallen waste. Behind the outhouse on the exterior should be a hinged trapdoor so that you can pull out the bucket to dispose of the waste. One good method is to burn it.

Another good technique for males to urinate is to take some PVC pipe about six to eight feet in length and bury it in the ground at about a forty-five-degree angle. Take some metal screening such as that you would find on a porch, and use it to cover the opening by securing it with a zip tie or hose clamp. This will allow you to urinate through the screen, down the pipe, and into the ground without allowing flies and critters to live inside, which otherwise could give you a surprise in the middle of the night. If you are ever camping or in a survival situation long term in the woods, dig a trench about two feet deep with all the dirt piled up on one side. As you work your way down the trench, using it for number one or number two, you can fill it in as you go so that your campsite doesn't stink and attract attention.

13

WEAPONS

One of the greatest struggles for Christians is knowing when or how to defend themselves. Some Christians may not even be sure if it is acceptable by God to defend themselves. I'm sure that most people have heard of the scripture in Matthew 5:39 where Jesus commands us to "turn the other cheek." It's important to know that this scripture is meant as an admonishment not to retaliate against our enemies for petty insults such as verbal jabs, slaps, and disputes. Jesus continues on from there to say that you are to love your enemies, bless those who curse you, do good to those who hate you, and pray for those who persecute you.

As a soldier and a war fighter, I sometimes remembered to pray for my enemies as it was something that I was taught as a child. As difficult as it was for me at times, I remembered to pray that my enemies would turn to the one true God and follow Jesus. I also prayed that if they still chose to fight, God would give me the strength and the ability to successfully do what I'd been trained to do in war. This is very important: at no point in the Bible does it say that you should let your enemies persecute you and kill you. In Matthew 5:10 it says that those who are persecuted for righteousness' sake are blessed, not that you should aim to be persecuted. The Bible never forbids Christians from owning a weapon and never tells Christians that if they do own a weapon, they should get rid of it or destroy it. In the book Luke, after Peter cut off the ear of one of the servants of the high priest who came to arrest Jesus, he was not told to get rid of his sword. Instead he was told to put the sword away, that "now is not the time." Jesus also has the authority to send legions of angels to fight on His behalf if He commands them to.

> **And He said to them, "When I sent you without money bag, knapsack, and sandals, did you lack anything?"**
>
> **So they said, "Nothing."**
>
> **Then He said to them, "But now, he who has a money bag, let him take it, and likewise a knapsack; and he who has no sword, let him sell his garment and buy one. For I say to you that this which is written must still be accomplished in Me: 'And He was numbered with the transgressors.' For the things concerning Me have an end."**
>
> **So they said, "Lord, look, here are two swords."**

And He said to them, "It is enough." (Luke 22:35–38)

The first time that Jesus sent His disciples out to minister was to test their faith and their trust in God to provide for them while they carried out their mission. The severity of their discipleship would change as a result of Judas's betrayal. Jesus knew that He was about to be taken away, and He wanted His disciples to be prepared for the upcoming events. Jesus knew that He was about to be considered an outlaw and that His followers needed to be prepared as they soon would be pooled in that same category.

In those days when travelers prepared for a journey, they would bring a double-edged sword to defend themselves against bandits and robbers, which were common on the roads. Also, travelers would bring a shorter, single-edged blade for use as a tool for cutting that was also able to be used for self-defense. I believe that when the disciples said, "Here are two swords," they were speaking about each individual person in their group, saying they had both a sword and a smaller blade so as to give a response to the question about their level of readiness.

Like the disciples in this scripture, we are to be ready to defend ourselves and our loved ones against persecution. At no point in this scripture did Jesus say that we are to prepare to be on the warpath and have a desire to kill our enemies during our ministry. We still need to trust that God will provide for us and that we will live peaceful lives. However, we are also not to be weak and cowardly or allow ourselves to roll over and be killed and persecuted either.

"Let every soul be subject to the governing authorities. For there is no authority except from God, and the authorities that exist are appointed by God" (Romans 13:1).

As Christians we are not above the law. We must submit to the ruling authorities whom God appointed to rule and provide structure to our way of life. However, if the laws of our government contradict God's law, then it is our duty to resist and not violate God's will for us. It is our responsibility to defend the Christian way of life peacefully. Thankfully we have the ability in the United States to have a voice and make a difference when God's laws are violated.

"Therefore I exhort first of all that supplications, prayers, intercessions, and giving of thanks be made for all men, for kings and all who are in authority, that we may lead a quiet and peaceable life in all godliness and reverence. For this is good and acceptable in the sight of God our Savior, who desires all men to be saved and to come to the knowledge of the truth" (1 Timothy 2:1–2).

God desires for every man, woman, and child to accept Christ and be saved. God's will on earth was never for us to be in pain and suffer or to kill one another. Because of sin, death and sickness are able to exist on earth. Ezekiel 18:23 says that God does not take pleasure in punishing the wicked.

As Christians, it is our duty to pray for the people who don't know Christ. It is our duty to share the Word of God with nonbelievers and to share God's love. Jesus's sacrifice was meant for everyone on earth so that they could receive God's grace. So when you see a nonbeliever who isn't behaving like a Christian, it is not your right to look down on that person in an attempt to feel better about yourself or think that you are such a great Christian. Instead of being disgusted with that individual, you should be willing to look at him or her with compassion and be ready to war spiritually against whatever evil spirit has established a foothold in that person's life. I believe that this is one of the most difficult things for Christians, including me, to do in their lives and that it should be prayed about constantly.

"All things are lawful for me, but not all things are helpful; all things are lawful for me, but not all things edify. Let no one seek his own, but each one the other's well-being" (1 Corinthians 10:23).

Whatever you are doing in your life, you should always ask yourself, "Does it honor God and express His will on earth?" We should be focused on uplifting each other's spirits with unconditional love and encouragement. Of course, if every Christian in the world were to do this, we would be that much closer to everything being fine and dandy. Now ask yourself this: does your owning a weapon of some sort honor God and cause His will to be done on earth? Well, for police officers and military personnel, that's a pretty easy question to answer because weapons are some of the tools of their trade. Without law enforcement to maintain peace and a military to defend our nation against foreign enemy attacks, there would be no peace. But what about for the everyday civilian? Matthew 5:9 says, "Blessed are the peacemakers, for they shall be called sons of God."

Do you know that the most violent crimes that are committed in the United States occur in places where the citizens are not allowed to own firearms or other weapons? The most dangerous places in the United States of America are in gun-free zones! If you do not believe me, do the research. You will be amazed. It's common sense to comprehend that the bad guys of the world are willing to prey on the defenseless and avoid those who are equipped to protect themselves. So now ask yourself, does owning a weapon help maintain peace and honor God? I'd say that should be a pretty solid yes.

You shall not murder. (Exodus 20:13)

Now we know that whatever the law says, it says to those who are under the law, that every mouth may be stopped, and all the world may become guilty before God. Therefore by the deeds of the law no flesh will be justified in His sight, for by the law is the knowledge of sin. (Romans 3:19–20)

Many people have been misled over the years to believe that this scripture translates as, "Thou shall not *kill*—period." However, the actual Hebrew word for *kill* in this verse means "murder." Murder is the intentional, premeditated killing of another person with malice. In other words, there is justified and unjustified killing. Consider it this way: thou shall not kill unlawfully, resulting in guilt.

As Christians, we have an obligation to follow a moral law that is written and explained in the

Word of God. At the end of the day, we are all guilty in the sight of the Lord because of the knowledge of sin. According to human-made law, if you defend yourself and kill someone, you need to prove that you were in fear for your life or in fear of being permanently injured or maimed if you want to avoid a murder charge. When soldiers fight in a war, they have to legal right to kill an enemy combatant. However, as previously stated in 3, war fighters are required to follow the rules of engagement to ensure legal justification.

So it behooves you to know for a fact, without a shadow of a doubt, that the person you intend to use a firearm against is threatening your life or the lives of your family or other law-abiding citizens around you. Of course I am not a legal professional. If you have any further questions regarding this topic, I advise you to seek the counsel of a legal professional. Find someone who is a subject matter expert on this topic of the law in whichever state you may reside.

To everything there is a season,

    A time for every purpose under heaven;

    A time to kill,

    And a time to heal;

    A time to break down,

    And a time to build up; ...

    A time to love,
    And a time to hate;

> A time of war,
> And a time of peace.
> —Ecclesiastes 3:1, 3, 8

> You are My battle-ax and weapons of war:
> For with you I will break the nation in pieces;
> With you I will destroy kingdoms.
> —Jeremiah 51:20

We know that the world we live in is riddled with sin and hate. War is an inevitable result of human nature because of sin. In fact, if anyone promises that they will bring or have brought peace on earth, be leery because only Jesus can bring peace on earth. Peace will arrive after the battle of Armageddon takes place and only after Satan is cast into the lake of fire, which is after the great tribulation.

Although we pray for our enemies, we are also ready to fight to protect our nation from being besieged by evil. War is necessary to prevent a greater evil from emerging. War is why the Nazis are not still killing Jewish people in concentration camps. War is why the United States no longer enslaves African Americans. The global war on terrorism is why US soldiers were able to do battle against terrorists off US soil to disrupt further plots against the United States.

War can be extremely harsh, and it is not kind. Just like God does not take pleasure in punishing the wicked, a soldier, especially a Christian soldier, should not take pleasure in killing his or her enemies. Soldiers are, however, duty bound to kill in combat and should be honored to fight for their country on the battlefield. Although there is a time and a place for war and killing, Christians should pray for the safety of the civilian noncombatants and that the conflict will end with haste.

> **Blessed be the Lord my Rock,**
> **Who trains my hands for war,**
> **And my fingers for battle.**
> —Psalm 144:1

Rangers are trained to use their hands as weapons and their weapons as hands. Anything and everything can be used as a weapon if need be. When David took on Goliath, he turned down the sword and shield because it was too heavy for him and slew the giant with a sling and a rock. Throughout the history of the world, humans have depended on weapons to survive and defend themselves or their homes against others who would do harm.

The Second Amendment to the United States Constitution reads, "A well-regulated Militia, being necessary to the security of a free State, the right of the people to keep and bear Arms, shall not be infringed." Today many law-abiding US citizens still depend on weapons and practice using weapons, exercising their Second Amendment rights. There is much controversy in today's society as to whether or not the average US citizen should be allowed to carry weapons (mainly concerning firearms), and if so in what manner.

I believe that (1) we have the God-given right as Americans to carry or bear arms, (2) there will always be evil people readily available within every culture around the world who inevitably and eventually will use either a firearm or a horrendous type of weaponry to do harm to the innocent, and (3) different weapons/firearms are a great resource for hunting as previously stated in *Millennial Ranger*.

In regard to firearms, there is much debate concerning certain limitations that should be applied to their use by the average law-abiding US citizen. Of these debates, the most frequent are rate of fire, magazine/ammo capacity, silencer/suppresser, and the size of the firearm, specifically the length of the barrel. I for one don't see a problem with allowing these features to be limitlessly optional without any further extreme regulations. Yes, you don't need thirty rounds or more to kill a deer; however, one day you could possibly need thirty rounds or more to prevent an attack by invading foreign soldiers or tyrannical forces led by our own government. Is it anti-American or antigovernment to think this way? No, it is one of the most American-driven ways of thinking that is derived all the way from the birth of our nation as a result of the Revolutionary War. People have fought and died to preserve this God-given right.

Most people who are against everyday carry (EDC) for civilians will point out that if you are not a professional law enforcement officer or military war fighter, you don't need certain upgraded features on a firearm. Perhaps they are right to a certain extent; however, how many people who are not professional racecar drivers own a vehicle that can reach a maximum speed of 120 mph when, on average, the highest speed limits on the freeway only range from 55 mph to 75 mph? I would also like to point out that more Americans die because of vehicle negligence than because of firearm negligence. Perhaps the people who are anti-Second Amendment wouldn't mind giving up their cars for a ride that can only go up to 55 mph. And if they get special permission and go through a lengthy application process, they can upgrade to a higher level of classification that allows them to drive a car that goes 75 mph. Then they have to undergo another lengthy application process that will afford them the right to own speakers that have the capability to produce sound greater than 65 decibels. In addition, they will have to write a form and wait a month or so for a response from the government granting them permission to take their vehicle to another state.

Firearms are the most common and modern type of weaponry available in modern American society. There are several different types of firearms that vary with all sorts of capabilities and specifications. Different firearms afford better results in different types of situations. I believe that there is no one firearm that is best for all situations. Also, in addition to the different types of firearms, there is great variety in weapons caliber. So, not only is there no one firearm, but also there is no one caliber that would serve as a "silver bullet" in a survival situation (pun intended).

If there is one thing that I have discovered in all my research into the varieties of firearms, it's that no matter what the topic, whether firearm type, caliber, or even manufacturer, not everyone is going to appreciate the same things in firearms. There are people out there who actually have some pretty good ideas regarding firearm type and caliber. Others have horrible ideas. The bottom line is, firearms come in all different shapes and sizes.

There are several books written about firearms that go into great detail, extending well beyond my knowledge. I recommend seeking as much information about different firearms as you can if you intend on owning and using firearms. Also, ensure that you are not in violation of any federal or state laws.

Here is a basic list of the different categories of firearms: rifle, shotgun, and handgun. Within these categories are different types. For rifles, some common types are bolt action, semiautomatic, lever action, and muzzleloader. For shotguns, the common types are break action, pump action, and semiautomatic. The two main types of handguns or pistols are revolvers and semiauto. Semiauto pistols are either hammer fired or striker fired (double or single action). Revolvers can either be double action or single action as well.

It is my belief that if you are going to include firearms as part of your preparations, you shouldn't limit yourself to just one type. Think of firearms as what they actually are: tools. Not every problem is a nail, so not every tool or solution is a hammer. If you need a firearm for concealed carry, you would be best served by a pistol versus a rifle or a shotgun (both of which are illegal to conceal anyway). To be more precise, not all pistols can be concealed easily. In most cases you will want a subcompact pistol that holds anywhere from seven to ten rounds depending on caliber. Some people are more comfortable carrying just a little bit larger compact pistol that can hold around twelve to fifteen rounds. I've known people to carry full-size pistols as their EDC that hold thirteen to seventeen rounds.

I believe that above all other firearms, the most crucial firearm for survival is a concealed handgun for self-defense and deterring persecution. During the tribulation, if you are spotted by people who have accepted the mark of the beast carrying a rifle or a shotgun, you will stick out as someone who hasn't bought into the system and will be targeted for persecution. If the situation dictates, at the very least you should always have a handgun ready as a "get off me" tool so you can get away.

For beginners it can be a challenge trying to decipher what type of firearms will meet your needs. Firearm types, calibers, and sizes can be quite a headache even for people who have some experience and know what they are looking for. My advice is to use the acronym KISS: keep it simple, stupid. Try not to overthink what you are trying to accomplish. Here is a list of basic, well-rounded weapons that most people acquire by precedence:

1. A 9 mm compact pistol—a good, well-rounded self-defense firearm that can be effective for both concealed carry / EDC and home defense. A good choice for a secondary weapon.
2. A twelve-gauge pump-action shotgun—a well-rounded and reliable firearm capable of shooting different sizes of "shot" for harvesting different game. Also effective for home defense.
3. A .308 bolt-action rifle—a traditional hunting round capable of taking down large game at a long distance. Sniper rifles are based on

this rifle type and caliber and are equipped with high-powered scopes.
4. A .22-caliber rifle, either bolt-action or semiautomatic—a great choice for harvesting small game. It can be used for self-defense but is not the best choice against armed attacks.
5. A 5.56 × 45/7.62 × 51/7.62 × 39 semiautomatic rifle—AR-15, AR-10, and AK-47 rifles are great and are ideal for survival and self-defense situations. They can use high-capacity magazines and are good for hunting game. The AR-15 is the civilian version of the rifle that is currently in common use by the US military. Ideal for a primary weapon system.

I believe that you should pick your favorite primary firearm and favorite secondary firearm and be as proficient with those specific two weapon systems as you can. The reason you want to be the most proficient with those two firearms is that you will not be able to carry several firearms with you at all times. Also, carrying a plethora of different types of ammo to sustain the usefulness of these weapons will prove to be extremely heavy and counterproductive. You are more likely to run out of different types of ammo quickly—and without ammunition, firearms simply become paperweights.

If you are having a hard time deciding for yourself which primary and which secondary weapon systems you should go with, welcome to the club! I would say that for beginners, the AR-15 and the 9 mm compact pistol go very well together for well-roundedness. This is the same combination that most military and law enforcement personnel are equipped with. Of course some people may want a larger primary and secondary weapon as their go-to weapons combination. There are many factors to consider, such as whether the firearm will be used to hunt, defend against large animals, or defend against humans. Ultimately the choice is yours, and the journey to discovering what works best for you is what will really shape your perspective. In the end, practical and safe training trumps everything else when it comes to self-defense firearms. If you don't know how to safely use whatever firearm you pick up, then it doesn't matter what you have in your arsenal, because you will not be effective with your weapon. Get out and shoot and see for yourself which firearm works best for you.

Four Safety Rules of Proper Gun Handling:
1. Treat all firearms as if they were loaded.
2. Never let your muzzle/gun point at anything you are not willing to destroy.
3. Keep your finger off the trigger until you have your target in your sights and you are ready to shoot.
4. Be cognizant of your target and what is behind it.

And remember to always keep your firearms locked and away from people whom you don't want to handle them to prevent crime and/or accidental death!

14

FAMILY AND COMMUNITY

One of the most important and defining key features of any special operations unit is the ability to carefully select members from a pool of potential candidates. The selection process is usually filled with rigorous physical and mental challenges that tempt and pressure candidates to either quit or fail. The reason for this isn't to make the candidates physically or mentally stronger but to figure out who will quit on their teammates, which become like family, and who will perform honorably when things get sketchy or out of control in real-life combat. Combat is often defined as controlled chaos. In these types of units, you want to be working with people who have displayed that they are of high caliber in soldiering techniques. That is what makes the 75th Ranger Regiment a great community to be a part of.

The most important thing to your physical and spiritual survival on earth is your family and the community that your family is part of. Your immediate family and your extended family is the foundation of your success. Your family is capable of doing great things for God when they all come together. When people come together and work as one unit, they are more capable of accomplishing physical things on earth as well.

The church is the family of God. There is no other family like it in the entire world. All the way back in the beginning, God created Adam, and He created Eve so that Adam would not be alone. It is important to God that we are not alone, which means that it should be important to you as well. And if you do ever get stranded or find yourself separated, remember that God is always with you (Deuteronomy 31:8). During the tribulation it will be critical to our mission to establish churches within our communities to do God's will.

> "So God created man in His own image; in the image of God He created him; male and female He created them. Then God blessed them, and God said to them, 'Be fruitful and multiply; fill the earth and subdue it; have dominion over the fish of the sea, over the birds of the air, and over every living thing that moves on the earth'" (Genesis 1:27–28).

As Christians, we are blessed by God and commanded to be fruitful and multiply. He loves us so much that He trusts us to have dominion over the earth. Because we are blessed and God does not want us to be alone, we are to raise up other Christians. Our children are our legacies, but so are the other people we bring to Christ. One way or another it is God's will that we be part of a family that is set up to glorify our Creator.

> **Now it came to pass, when men began to multiply on the face of the earth, and daughters were born to them, that the sons of God saw the daughters of men, that they were beautiful; and they took wives for themselves of all whom they chose.**
>
> **And the Lord said, "My Spirit shall not strive with man forever, for he is indeed flesh; yet his days shall be one hundred and twenty years." There were giants on the earth in those days, and also afterward, when the sons of God came in to the daughters of men and they bore children to them. Those were mighty men who were of old, men of renown. (Genesis 6:1-4)**

When the fallen angels (sons of God) bred with the daughters of men, that was a diabolical plan of Satan to try to corrupt the bloodline of the Messiah way before Jesus was born. The giants that were created as a result of this interbreeding were abominations called the Nephilim. They were violent and took part in cannibalism. This is why God allowed the Flood in the book of Genesis to occur. God used Noah and his family to preserve the bloodline because Noah found grace in the eyes of the Lord (Genesis 6:8). While everything else was wiped out by the flood, Noah's family and the animals that God created were spared because they still had a pure bloodline. Later on, after the floodwaters were gone, God commanded Noah and his sons to be fruitful and multiply and fill the earth, just like He'd commanded Adam and Eve (Genesis 9:1).

> **"For the Lord God of Israel says**
> **That He hates divorce,**
> **For it covers one's garment with violence,"**
> **Says the Lord of hosts.**
> **"Therefore take heed to your spirit,**
> **That you do not deal treacherously."**
> **—Malachi 2:16**
>
> **A wife is bound by law as long as her husband lives; but if her husband dies, she is at liberty to be married to whom she wishes, only in the Lord. (1 Corinthians 7:39)**

Family is so important to God that He hates divorce. Marriage is a beautiful gift from God that should not be taken lightly. In today's US culture, marriage is at best a joke to many people. The American family has been under attack from the enemy for quite some time now. That is because Satan knows that a family devoted to God is capable of doing many great things when they are in the Spirit. The devil tries to distract families from accomplishing their most important role on earth: to do the will of God.

In Matthew 19:6, Jesus said that once a man and a woman are married, they are no longer two but one flesh. One of today's most common phrases of the wedding vows is, "Till death do us part." It was, and still is, God's intention for one man to be married to only one woman for life. According to the laws of scripture, only when a person's spouse dies are they legally allowed to remarry, that is, if that person is a man or woman devoted to God.

> **Train up a child in the way he should go, and when he is old he will not depart from it. (Proverbs 22:6)**
>
> **And you, fathers, do not provoke your children to wrath, but bring them up in the training and admonition of the Lord. (Ephesians 6:4)**

It is the responsibility of a parent to raise godly children. Good parenting applies all the teachings of the Bible to ensure that the children are prepared for the things to come later on in life. It is no guarantee that children will be godly if you raise them that way, which is why you need to plant good seeds in your children's life and rebuke in the name of Jesus the tares that the enemy has sown in their lives. Children are the legacy of their parents, and God wants mothers and fathers to be fruitful with their inheritance.

Having a good relationship with your children today will result in a great payoff tomorrow during an emergency when you absolutely need your child's attention and trust to follow you. Likewise, your experiences with raising your children also allow you to have a greater understanding of God the Father and how He disciplines and rewards His children. Good parents are patient and don't berate or yell at their children to achieve results. Good parents don't allow their children to have everything they want or reward bad behavior, because that would stunt the child's maturity. God wants our spiritual maturity to be fully grown.

> **But the mercy of the Lord is from everlasting to everlasting**
> **On those who fear Him,**
> **And His righteousness to children's children,**
> **To such as keep His covenant,**
> **And to those who remember His commandments to do them.**
> **—Psalm 103:17–18**

Your obedience to God today will bring on a blessing that will affect your children, their children, and their children's children. Likewise, disobedience can transfer generationally. It is important to be good role models of faith to your own kids or any other kids in your life. This isn't just for the sake of tradition but is for the sake of passing on God's blessings as you lead by example—an example not just to children but also to new Christians who are looking for leadership so that they can learn and one day become leaders themselves.

> **For we do not wrestle against flesh and blood, but against principalities, against powers, against the rulers of darkness of this age, against spiritual hosts of wickedness in the heavenly places. (Ephesians 6:12)**

For if you forgive men their trespasses, your heavenly Father will also forgive you. But if you do not forgive men their trespasses, neither will your Father forgive your trespasses. (Matthew 6:14-15)

Many families are going through some troubled times internally. Family feuds are the result of a successful attack carried out by Satan's minions. When you are going through a family dispute, it is important to understand that your family is under attack by evil spirits and principalities that reside in heavenly places and on the earth. The good news is that you and your family can easily overpower these demons by maintaining constant discipline in prayer.

If you are truly in the Spirit and are a follower of Christ, you will set aside your differences and simply forgive, even if forgiveness is not yet asked for. God forgave us of our sins before we were even born into this world. Because Christ forgave us, we should forgive others (Colossians 3:13). Sometimes all it takes is for one member of a family to pray and forgive to begin the counterattack against influential demons.

> "And let us consider one another in order to stir up love and good works, not forsaking the assembling of ourselves together, as is the manner of some, but exhorting one another, and so much the more as you see the Day approaching" (Hebrews 10:24-25).

As the great and terrible day of the Lord

approaches, we should be stirring up a Holy Spirit revival with those around us. Never should we look down upon or turn our backs on nonbelievers. Instead, we should urge these people toward love and good works. We should pray for and with each other to provoke discipline and obedience to God.

> **For as the body is one and has many members, but all the members of that one body, being many, are one body, so also is Christ. For by one Spirit we were all baptized into one body—whether Jews or Greeks, whether slaves or free—and have all been made to drink into one Spirit. For in fact the body is not one member but many. ... And if one member suffers, all the members suffer with it, or if one member is honored, all the members rejoice with it. (1 Corinthians 12:12-15, 26)**

As children of God, we are all part of one family. And God wants us to congregate and work together to achieve His will. We are all exclusively connected with one another just by having all been blessed by the same Spirit. Just like the human body, all the unique parts of the Spirit must work together in order to function properly and remain in good health.

If you get injured, whether it's your foot, your hand, or something internal, overall it makes your normal way of living more difficult. When you maintain good health by eating properly, sleeping properly, and properly exercising all the muscles in your body, you are conditioned to be able to perform at your maximum potential.

"I fed you with milk and not with solid food; for until now you were not able to receive it, and even now you are still not able; for you are still carnal. For where there are envy, strife, and divisions among you, are you not carnal and behaving like mere men" (1 Corinthians 3:2–3)?

The milk of faith entails the very basics of being a Christian. As a baby grows into a toddler, it moves from milk to solid food. Just like a baby, new Christians should know the basics first and then desire to grow into the spiritual meat of the Word. However, if you are still bickering over things of the flesh, you are not consuming spiritual meat. If you boast about your ability to eat meat, you are really still in the milk stages. Both spiritual milk and meat are good for faith, especially when consumed together and in good company.

Whether it's a natural disaster or the breakdown of society, it will make things much more difficult if you have the mind-set that it's just you versus the entire world. There are people out there who have already set in motion the off-grid lifestyle. Other people, however, are accustomed to living as part of a system that has been emplaced to sustain a way of life. As functioning members of society, we are heavily reliant upon the relationships we form in order to survive. When this system is no longer present and the Antichrist establishes a new system, what then? It will ultimately be up to Christians to establish a system entirely based upon what God wills for us. This will be the key to our success. The church and our families will be the basis of this system. Essentially it will be no different from the early church days during the time of the apostle Paul.

Establishing and protecting a network of Christian communities will be paramount for the church. Either joining or starting your own neighborhood watch is a great way to be proactive in keeping your community safe and informed. A watch group is an association of neighbors who look out for each other's families and property. They alert the police to any suspicious activities or crimes in progress they may witness.

A team of volunteers should be responsible for relaying information to neighborhood watch members on their block, keeping up-to-date information on residents and making special efforts to involve all the members of the community in watching out for one another. These volunteers can also serve as liaisons between the neighborhood and the local police department. At the very least, members should attend meetings just to stay informed. All in all, a neighborhood watch group is able to work together to make their community a safer and better place to live.

One important thing for the effectiveness of these communities is location. I believe that the farther away you are from urban areas, the better off you will be. If you think about it, major cities in the United States already revolve around the latest system set up for people to make their lives more organized that leans toward getting people "on the same page." If people are already conditioned not to be self-sustaining, how do you think the transfer will go when the Antichrist sets up his new system? I imagine seamlessly. Not only do you want to be set up to maintain distance from this system, but also you want to be in an area that allows more opportunity to homestead and hunt as you will not be able to purchase certain necessities without the mark of the beast. Of course if you do live in an urban area, you have the opportunity to reach out to people and spread the good word. However, you should always be ready to move. The important thing to remember is that you must be where God tells you to be and not go against where He intends to put you. Do you remember reading about Jonah and the whale? God will get you there one way or another, so it's better if you listen the first time.

No matter where you end up, your relationships matter. Whom you surround yourself and your family with matters. Everyone in your community has a blessing from God in order to do His will. Everyone has a part to play in doing good works and contributing to the sustainability of their Christian brothers and sisters in their community. If you are new to a rural community, it would be best to befriend and take the advice from locals such as farmers and other homesteaders. These are the types of people who will be able to help you get on your feet.

15

ULTIMATE SURVIVAL

As far as survival goes, it's very easy to get caught up in the best ways to do things to make sure that you have all your bases covered—and rightfully so. In the military the saying goes, "Don't expect what you don't inspect," meaning that if you just assume something will be taken care of and you don't check on it yourself, the blame literally falls on you for not being a good leader if something isn't up to standard.

As a people going about our normal everyday lives, we all have goals, ambitions, and hobbies that distract us from the things of the world such as politics and work. We are competitive by nature and want to be the best at the things we do. If staying alive is the key issue in what we have going on, it's very easy to view the world through the eyes of the flesh and forget about the lens of the Spirit.

Because it is inevitable that the human body will expire, we should let God be our ultimate distraction from the world. Jesus said, "And do not fear those who kill the body but cannot kill the soul. But rather fear Him who is able to destroy both soul and body in hell" (Matthew 10:28-29).

> **For you were bought at a price; therefore glorify God in your body and in your spirit, which are God's. (1 Corinthians 6:20)**
>
> **No one can serve two masters; for either he will hate the one and love the other, or else he will be loyal to the one and despise the other. You cannot serve God and mammon. (Matthew 6:24)**

When you choose to serve God, your physical body and your spirit are used to glorify God as you do His will. This life does not belong to you. It was bought and paid for by the blood of Jesus Christ. Only by the grace of God through the sacrifice of Jesus are you saved.

If you believe in Jesus, you should be all in without any feelings of insecurity, embarrassment, or doubt. There is nothing ambiguous about the fact that you cannot serve two masters and still be called a Christian. The excuses that people create for themselves to give in to temptation are not legitimate alibies; they are self-destructive acts of sin that ultimately lead to death. However, when you do serve the one true God, you have everything you need for eternal life.

> "Who Himself bore our sins in His own body on the tree, that we, having died to sins, might live for righteousness—by

whose stripes you were healed" (1 Peter 2:24).

Not only did Jesus come to save us from our sins, which results in death, but He also came to heal us. We are already healed, and it is not God's plan for us to be sick or suffering. Satan and his demons want to take the good things in your life away from you by trying to make you sick. The devil wants to tempt you into making bad decisions that lead to more suffering in your life. There is literally a battle for your life and your soul. There is an invisible war going on around you. Whether you like it or not, you are a part of that war. It is your responsibility to war against these things in the Spirit and not in the flesh. You are not capable of fighting spiritual warfare on your own, but the Holy Spirit does things through you. As a follower of Christ, you have the power of the Holy Spirit within you to do God's will. Romans 8:11 says that the Spirit that rose Jesus from the dead is the same Spirit that is in those who believe in Him and worship God.

"Now when Daniel knew that the writing was signed, he went home. And in his upper room, with his windows open toward Jerusalem, he knelt down on his knees three times that day, and prayed and gave thanks before his God, as was his custom since early days" (Daniel 6:10).

Daniel remained obedient to God and prayed consistently at the expense of encountering a great amount of physical danger. The king had been tricked into creating a law stating that to worship any other god instead of him was a crime punishable by death. This ultimately led to Daniel being thrown in the lions' den, a scriptural story that most people are familiar with. Because of Daniel's obedience, he continued to pray and worship God even when it put his own life in jeopardy. God rescued Daniel and continued to bless him and use him to do His will.

Prayer is the key ingredient of anything we do in our lives. Obedience in prayer is your connection to God in heaven that brings on revelation from the Holy Spirit. When we are filled with the Spirit, it gives us the ability to interpret scripture found in the Bible. Reading the Word of God is how you establish a personal relationship with Jesus. Without reading and understanding His Word, how can you know what His will truly is for you on this earth? How can you know the things that He did for you while He was alive on this earth? The Bible is how you know what is supposed to be going on in your life according to your most important friend and ally, Jesus.

"For the word of God is living and powerful, and sharper than any two-edged sword, piercing even to the division of soul and spirit, and of joints and marrow, and is a discerner of the thoughts and intents of the heart" (Hebrews 4:12).

The Word of God is a sword to be used against the enemy. Evil spirits and principalities know the scriptures and will try to twist it to push their agenda, just like when Satan tempted Jesus in the wilderness. It is up to you to know the true meaning of the scriptures and to put on the whole armor of God so that you can effectively do His will and combat evil. The living Word of God is a powerful tool that can allow you to discern between what is of the flesh and what is of the Spirit. It even has the ability to pierce through to the core of the enemy to effectively destroy them. These things in the Word of God are not just metaphors to maintain your interest and get you excited with inspiration; they are literally real tools that God gives you to fight real battles. Use the gift of discernment that God gave you and scan the battlefield through the lens of the Spirit so that you will never be deceived by the enemy.

> "For many will come in My name, saying, 'I am the Christ,' and will deceive many" (Matthew 24:5).

When the Antichrist tries to set up his kingdom on earth, you will need to be ready to avoid deception and prepare for the Truth (Jesus). Because you know Christ and you are a child of God, you will not fall for the counterfeit savior or the false prophets. You will not fall for the illusion of peace when there is really war. You will be ready to harvest souls for the one true God and to do His will on earth.

> **Not everyone who says to Me, "Lord, Lord," shall enter the kingdom of heaven, but he who does the will of My Father in heaven. Many will say to Me in that day, "Lord, Lord, have we not prophesied in Your name, cast out demons in Your name, and done many wonders in Your name?" And then I will declare to them, "I never knew you; depart from Me, you who practice lawlessness!" (Matthew 7:21-23)**

> **But we are all like an unclean thing, And all our righteousnesses are like filthy rags;**

We all fade as a leaf,
And our iniquities, like the wind,
Have taken us away.

—Isaiah 64:6

Therefore we make it our aim, whether present or absent, to be well pleasing to Him. For we must all appear before the judgment seat of Christ, that each one may receive the things done in the body, according to what he has done, whether good or bad. Knowing therefore, the terror of the Lord, we persuade men; but we are well known to God, and I also trust are well known in your consciences. (2 Corinthians 5:9–11)

Then I saw a great white throne and Him who sat on it, from whose face the earth and the heaven fled away. And there was found no place for them. And I saw the dead, small and great, standing before God, and books were opened. And another book was opened, which is the Book of Life. And the dead were judged according to their works, by the things which were written in the books. The sea gave up the dead who were in it, and Death and Hades delivered up the dead who were in them. And they were judged, each one according to his works. Then Death and Hades were cast into the lake of fire. This is the second death. And anyone not found written in the Book

of Life was cast into the lake of fire. (Revelation 20:11–15)

Eventually we will all die unless we are raptured first. Either way, we are going to have to go before the Lord for judgment. No one from any religious background will have any doubt that the one who is judging them is Jesus Christ. Christians will appear before the judgment seat of Christ. Nonbelievers will appear before the great white throne of judgment. One group will be found in the Book of Life, whereas the other will not. Those of the latter group will be cast into the lake of fire forever.

When I was a kid, my dad asked me something that was, and still is, one of the wisest things I have ever been taught: "If you died and Jesus asked you why you should be allowed in heaven, what would you say to Him?" Of course I listed off all sorts of nice deeds that I usually did that would convince anyone that I was a good Christian boy. Then my dad proceeded to tell me, "No. The correct answer is, 'I don't deserve to be in heaven.'" At the time, for a moment, it felt like a cruel concept, but it's true: none of us deserve to be in heaven. Nonbelievers will want to list all the good deeds they did in life to try to convince Jesus that they are worthy to be in His kingdom. True children of God will recognize that their good deeds are like dirty rags compared to the sacrifice that Jesus made on the cross, knowing that faith in Jesus alone is their salvation.

"And do you think this, O man, you who judge those practicing such things, and doing the same, that you will escape the judgment of God? Or do you despise the riches of His goodness, forbearance, and longsuffering, not knowing that the goodness of God leads you to repentance? But in accordance with your hardness and your impenitent heart you are treasuring up for yourself wrath in the day of wrath and revelation of the righteous judgment of God, who 'will render to each one according to his deeds'" (Romans 2:3-6).

If you believe in Jesus, you will want to be judged not by your works but by His works! According to Romans 2:3-6, if you do not repent, you will suffer the wrath of God and your good deeds will be rendered useless. No matter who you are, you have sinned and therefore are not worthy to be in heaven.

> "And behold, I am coming quickly, and My reward is with Me, to give to every one according to his work. I am the Alpha and the Omega, the Beginning and the End, the First and the Last" (Revelation 22:12-13).

Jesus is coming back soon. The world may have less time than we think. There is going to be a shift in the spirit like never before during these approaching last days. We are hastening toward a decisive point in the war against evil. Time is running out to make important preparations. It is absolutely imperative to ready your soul and the souls of your loved ones. The whole Bible lays it out for us in plain sight. The Holy Spirit is ready to work through you in ways you could never imagine, and all you have to do is let Him in and listen. You have to bring Jesus into your life to receive a spiritual awakening. It is not just the most important thing; it is the only thing!

> "For the wages of sin is death, but the free gift of God is eternal life in Christ Jesus our Lord" (Romans 6:23).

If you are not saved, pray for forgiveness. If you are not sure where you are going when you die but you want to go to heaven, ask Jesus into your heart and let Him show you the way so that you don't just think you will go to heaven; you know without a shadow of a doubt that you will inherit God's kingdom. Allow Jesus to show you how to turn your life in the direction of God's will.

Repent of your sins; they have already been forgiven. Go before the Lord and give yourself to Him. Ask, and you shall receive salvation and grace from the Lord. Second Corinthians 5:17 says that if you are in Christ, you are a new creation and the old things that you have done have passed away.

Now is the time to make a change and become the person God created you to be! Now is the time to turn away from sin! Now is the time to cease being a victim of temptation! Now is the time to eschew being afraid of anything ever again! Now is the time to pick up your cross daily and follow Jesus! God loves you, and His Son Jesus Christ is the only way, the only truth, and the only life!

ABOUT THE AUTHOR

Christopher L. Watkins is a former Army Ranger and Special Operations Forces sniper. While assigned to Third Battalion, Seventy-Fifth Ranger Regiment, he fought and served during seven combat deployments to Iraq and Afghanistan. He enjoys spending time with his wife and two kids outdoors and at the beach.

As a homeschool dad, he is dedicated to teaching Bible study and history to his children. Driven by his faith in God and his unique experiences during his time in service, his life's mission is to help prepare people for Christ's return.

CPSIA information can be obtained
at www.ICGtesting.com
Printed in the USA
BVHW071414280821
615433BV00005B/658